easy

Microsoft® FrontPage® 2000

See it done

Do it yourself

que®

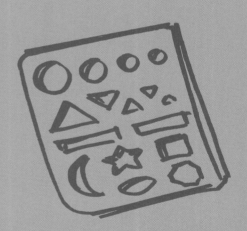

Easy Microsoft® FrontPage® 2000

Copyright © 1999 by Que® Corporation

International Standard Book Number: 0-7897-1807-3

Library of Congress Catalog Card Number: 98-88243

Printed in the United States of America

First Printing: May 1999

01 00 99   4   3   2   1

Trademarks

About the Author

Ned Snell has written many computer books and hundreds of articles on computing technology. He is the reviews editor for *Inside Technology Training* magazine, and he works as a professional actor in regional theater, commercials, and industrial films. He lives with his wife and two sons in Florida.

Dedication

For my family

Acknowledgments

Thanks to the folks at Macmillan Computer Publishing—especially Mark Taber, Pat Kinyon, and Carol Bowers.

Executive Editor
Mark Taber

Project Editor
Carol L. Bowers

Copy Editor
Patricia Kinyon

Technical Editor
Gina Carrilo

Indexer
Eric Schroeder

Proofreaders
Benjamin Berg
Gene Redding

Interior Design
Jean Bisesi

Cover Design
Anne Jones

Layout Technicians
Brian Borders
Susan Geiselman
Mark Walchle

How to Use This Book

It's as Easy as 1-2-3

Each part of this book is made up of a series of short, instructional lessons, designed to help you understand basic information that you need to get the most out of your computer hardware and software.

Click: Click the left mouse button once.

Double-click: Click the left mouse button twice in rapid succession.

Right-click: Click the right mouse button once.

Pointer Arrow: Highlights an item on the screen you need to point to or focus on in the step or task.

Selection: Highlights the area onscreen discussed in the step or task.

Click & Type: Click once where indicated and begin typing to enter your text or data.

(✓) Tips and **(!) Warnings** give you a heads-up for any extra information you may need while working through the task.

(2) Each task includes a series of quick, easy steps designed to guide you through the procedure.

(1) Each step is fully illustrated to show you how it looks onscreen.

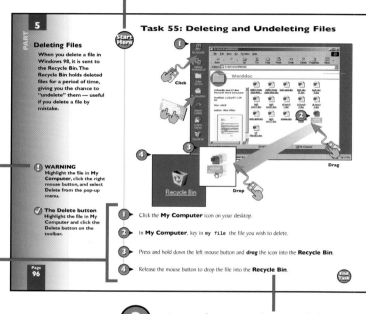

Task 55: Deleting and Undeleting Files

Deleting Files

When you delete a file in Windows 98, it is sent to the Recycle Bin. The Recycle Bin holds deleted files for a period of time, giving you the chance to "undelete" them — useful if you delete a file by mistake.

(!) WARNING
Highlight the file in **My Computer**, click the right mouse button, and select Delete from the pop-up menu.

(✓) The Delete button
Highlight the file in My Computer and click the Delete button on the toolbar.

(1) Click the **My Computer** icon on your desktop.

(2) In **My Computer**, key in my file the file you wish to delete.

(3) Press and hold down the left mouse button and *drag* the icon into the **Recycle Bin**.

(4) Release the mouse button to drop the file into the **Recycle Bin**.

Page 96

(3) Items that you select or click in menus, dialog boxes, tabs, and windows are shown in **Bold**. Information you type is in a `special font`.

How to Drag: Point to the starting place or object. Hold down the mouse button (right or left per instructions), move the mouse to the new location, then release the button.

Next Step: If you see this symbol, it means the task you're working on continues on the next page.

End Task: Task is complete.

Introduction to Easy Microsoft FrontPage 2000

If it's an easy Web authoring experience you're looking for, you've already done two things right. The first was choosing FrontPage 2000 as your Web authoring program. There are easier programs, but none that let you create really professional-looking pages and entire Web sites as easily.

Your second smart step in keeping things easy was picking up this book. Here, you'll find not only clear, simple steps for using FrontPage 2000 to create Web pages and make them look great, but also help with developing whole Web sites ("webs" in FrontPage-speak), publishing your page, and promoting it.

All you need to get started is your PC, access to the Internet, and FrontPage 2000 itself. (It's OK if you've already installed FrontPage, but if you haven't, you'll learn how in Part I.) Got all that? Okay, then it's time to get started…

PART 1

Getting Started with FrontPage 2000

Like all better Web authoring programs, FrontPage 2000 is described as a *WYSIWYG (what you see is what you get)* program, because while you're working on a Web page, the program shows you what the page will look like online. A WYSIWYG Web authoring program enables you to create a Web page in much the same way you would create a letter, brochure, or flyer on a word processor.

Then again, a Web authoring program is not exactly like any word processor you may already have met. So before diving into creating pages (as you'll do in Part 2, "Starting (and Saving) New Web Pages"), it's smart to spend a few, easy minutes now exploring the FrontPage program. This orientation will make everything that follows it even easier.

Tasks

Task 1: Setting Up FrontPage 2000

FrontPage is a snap to install. If you've set up other Windows 95, 98, or NT programs (especially those from Microsoft), you'll find installing FrontPage easy and familiar. (If you've already installed FrontPage 2000, skip to Task 2.)

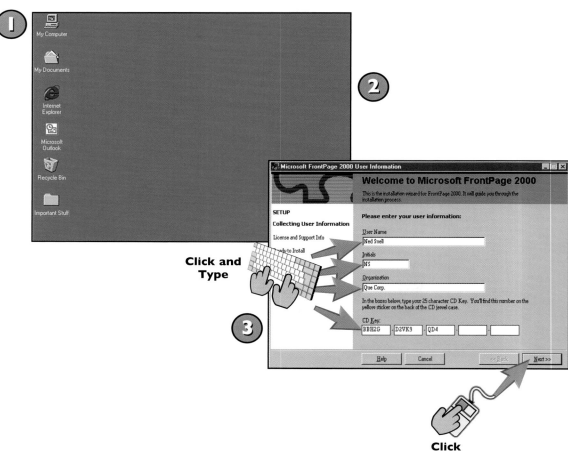

✓ If you got FrontPage along with your copy of Office 2000, install Office and select **FrontPage** when prompted to choose programs to install.

✓ The screen images in this book show FrontPage 2000 running in Windows 98. But it'll look and work the same in Windows 95 or NT, and all the steps you learn here work there, too.

1 Close all programs except Windows, and then insert the FrontPage 2000 CD-ROM.

2 Wait for Setup to start automatically. (If it doesn't, open your My Computer folder and double-click the **CD icon**.)

3 Fill in the blanks—including the CD key you'll find printed on the FrontPage CD-ROM case—and then click **Next**.

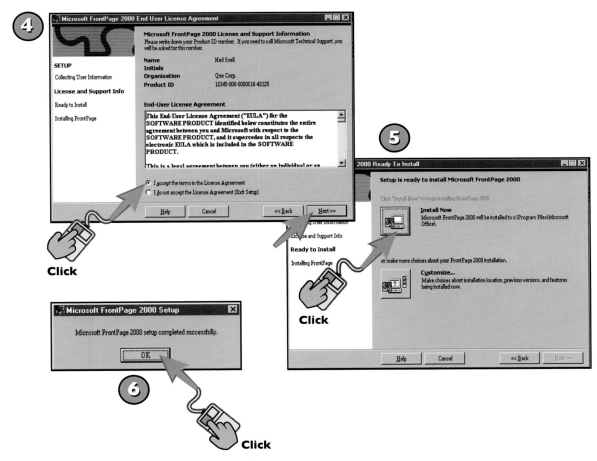

Click

Click

Click

In step 5, you can click the **Customize** button to choose which parts of FrontPage to install and which to ignore. But most users—and *all* beginners—should rely on the **Install Now** button. Down the road, you can repeat this task if you want to switch to a custom setup.

After setup, put your FrontPage CD-ROM away—the CD-ROM need not be in your PC when you use FrontPage. However, some activities—such as inserting *clip art* (see Part 6, "Adding and Formatting Pictures")—may require the CD-ROM, but when you begin these activities FrontPage reminds you to insert it.

4 Click **I accept the terms in the License Agreement**, and then click **Next**.

5 Click the **Install Now** button. Daydream while FrontPage completes Setup by itself—this may take 10–20 minutes.

6 When FrontPage reports that Setup is finished, click **OK**, and then click **Yes** when prompted to restart Windows.

End Task

Task 2: Opening FrontPage

Here's how to get FrontPage 2000 open and ready for work. Remember that even though the pictures here show Windows 98, the steps are the same whether you use Windows 98, Windows 95, or Windows NT.

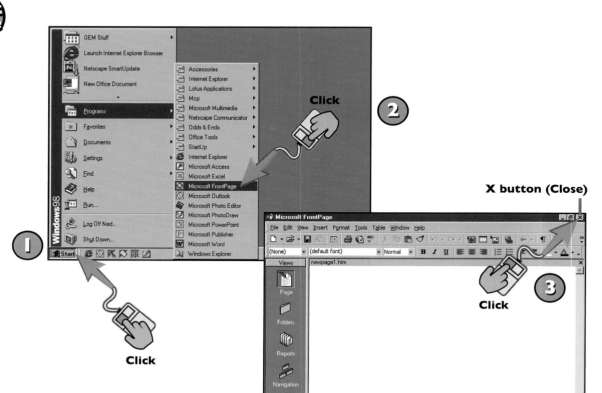

✓ When FrontPage opens, it automatically opens a new, blank Web page file. You can start typing right away to begin creating a Web page—although in Part 2, you'll discover better ways to get a new page going.

✓ You close FrontPage by clicking **File** and then choosing **Exit**, or by clicking the **X** button in the upper-right corner of the FrontPage window.

1 Click the Windows **Start** button.

2 Choose **Programs**, and then choose **Microsoft FrontPage**.

3 Click the **X button** in the upper-right corner to close FrontPage.

Task 3: Choosing a View

Page button

Click

Views bar

Click

FrontPage 2000 offers six different windows, or views, each of which is used for a different type of activity. You choose the view you want to work in by clicking a button in the *Views bar*. When creating and editing Web pages, you'll work mostly in Page view. The other five views are for managing Webs (multiple pages that work together to form a whole Web site), which you'll explore in Part 9, "Building a Web."

1. To switch from Page view to any other, click the appropriate button in the **Views bar**.

2. To return to Page view so you can work on Web pages, click the **Page button** in the **Views bar**.

3. To hide the Views bar (so you can see more of the page you're working on), choose **View**, and then **Views Bar** from the menu bar. To bring it back, choose **View**, **Views Bar** again.

✓ Try not to confuse the "Views bar" with the View menu on the menu bar.

✓ While the Views bar is hidden, you can switch among views by opening the **View menu** from the menu bar and then clicking the name of the view you want.

Task 4: Using Page View's Tabs

While you're in Page view, you'll notice three small tabs at the bottom of the work area: Normal, HTML, and Preview.

Start Here

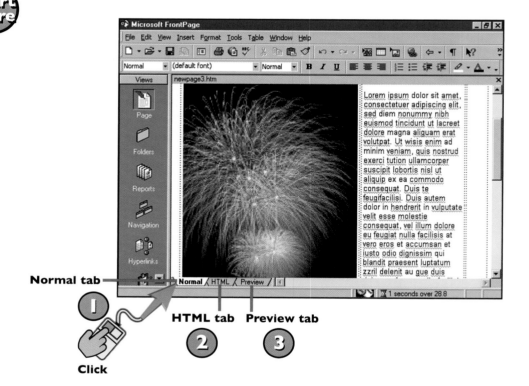

Normal tab

HTML tab   Preview tab

Click

①

②   ③

✓ **HTML** is the name for the underlying language in which Web pages are created. The Normal tab makes Web authoring easier by showing the page much as it will look online, while you work, hiding the raw HTML code. But advanced authors sometimes edit the code in the HTML tab to do things for which FrontPage offers no tools. Beginners can pretty much ignore the HTML tab.

① Click the **Normal** tab to open the space in which you create, edit, and format the contents of your page.

② Click the **HTML** tab to see the actual, raw *HTML* code of the page you're creating.

③ Click the **Preview** tab to see a close match to the way it would appear if viewed online through a Web browser (see Part 2), without the guidelines and other helpful objects displayed in the Normal tab.

End Task

Task 5: Identifying Toolbar Buttons

You perform many activities in FrontPage by clicking buttons on the **toolbars** that appear near the top of the window. The pictures in this book will help you easily identify and locate the toolbar button you need for any task, but it's also handy to know how to display ToolTips—pop-up labels—to learn the name of any button on a toolbar.

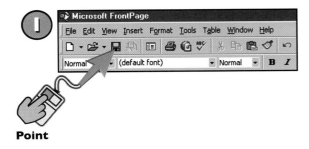

Point

① Point to the button whose name you want to know—but don't click.

② Wait a moment without moving the mouse, and the button's name appears.

To easily review the names on a whole row of buttons, point to the first button in the row and wait for its ToolTip to appear. Then slowly move the pointer to the right, along the row, without pausing. As the pointer passes each button, the button's name appears.

You perform most Web-page authoring activities with two main toolbars: the Standard toolbar and the Formatting toolbar. But FrontPage actually has seven more toolbars, most of which appear automatically when you need them and disappear when you don't (so they don't clutter up the screen). Still, anytime you need a particular toolbar and don't see it, you can make it appear.

To the far right of the toolbars, a tiny arrow sometimes appears. If you click that arrow and then click the button that appears, you can choose which tools appear on the toolbar. For now, it's best to leave the buttons as they are. But when you're ready, it's nice to know you can customize the toolbars to your precise needs.

Task 6: Choosing Which Toolbars to Display

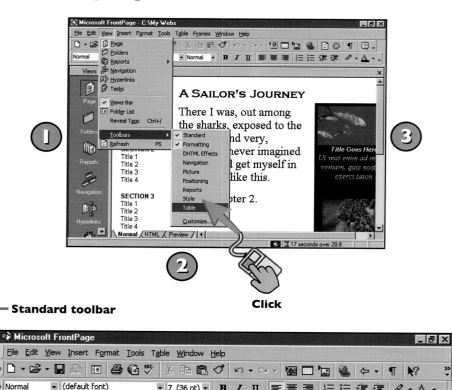

Standard toolbar

Formatting toolbar

Click

1 From the menu bar, choose **View**, **Toolbars**. In the submenu that appears, you'll see a check mark next to the name of each toolbar that's currently displayed.

2 To display a toolbar that's not checked, click its name in the submenu.

3 To hide a toolbar that is checked, click its name in the submenu.

Task 7: Arranging Toolbars

Start Here

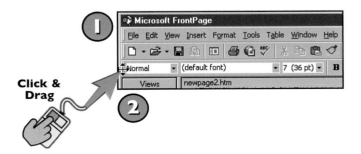

Click & Drag

You can move and rearrange FrontPage's toolbars in their "docked" positions above the work area, to change the top-to-bottom order in which they're shown. After some experience, you may find using the toolbars are more convenient if you rearrange their order in a way that best fits the way you work.

✓ You can also change the position of the FrontPage menu bar, following these same steps. For example, you can move the menu bar below the toolbars or between them.

✓ If you're not careful when dropping a toolbar in the toolbar area, you may overlap toolbars—put two on one line. Toolbars are overlapping when you see the (>>) in the middle of a row; clicking that symbol reveals the tools hidden by the overlapping. To fix the overlap, drag either toolbar a tiny way up or down.

① Point to the **vertical bar** at the extreme left end of the toolbar when docked above the workspace.

② Click and hold on the **vertical bar**, and then drag the toolbar up or down in the toolbar area to its new position.

③ Release the mouse button.

End Task

Task 8: Managing "Floating" Toolbars

A floating toolbar appears as a box of tools anywhere in the FrontPage window, not as a docked row in the toolbar area. You can float any toolbar (or even the menu bar), and you can drag a floating toolbar anywhere in the work area where it's both handy and out of your way. Some toolbars that appear automatically when needed (such as the Table toolbar; see Part 7, "Using Borders, Backgrounds, Sounds, and Other Fun Stuff") pop up as floaters, but you can dock those, too.

✓ Some toolbars, such as the Picture toolbar (see Part 6), pop up docked but not in the toolbar area—they dock below the work area. That's okay, but note that you can float these, too, or dock them in the toolbar area or on the sides.

✓ To easily "dock" a floating toolbar in the last place it was previously docked, double-click its **title bar**.

Start Here

Click

Drag

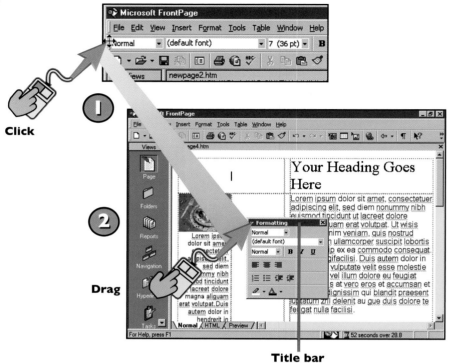

Title bar

Formatting toolbar

1 To float a toolbar, click and hold on its **vertical bar**, drag it onto the work area, and then release the mouse button.

2 To move a floating toolbar out of your way, click and hold on its **title bar** (where you see its name), and then drag it where you want it.

3 To dock a toolbar on the side or bottom of the screen, drag it all the way to the side or bottom.

End Task

Task 9: Undoing Mistakes

Start Here

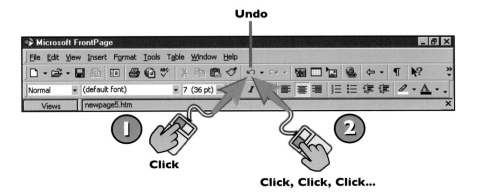

Undo

Click

Click, Click, Click...

Click

Here's as good a place as any to point out FrontPage's handy *Undo* feature. For example, if you delete some text or a picture and then suddenly realize that you want it back, you can use Undo to retrieve it. (When you get to where you're actually working in Web pages, I'll remind you about Undo.)

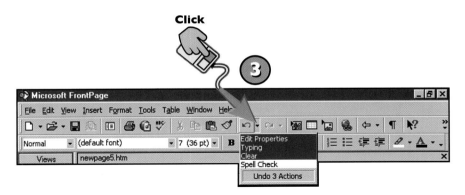

① Right after performing any action you regret, click the **Undo** button on the Standard toolbar to reverse that action.

② If you've performed several other actions since the action you want to undo, click **Undo** several times until the action is undone.

③ If you're not sure how many times to click Undo, click the **tiny arrow** on the right side of the Undo button to open a list of recent actions, and then click the bad one.

✅ When you click Undo several times to undo an action you made a little while ago, you undo not only that action, but *everything you've done since*—in effect, you take the page back in time to the moment before you goofed.

Task 10: Getting Help on a Topic

You can ask FrontPage 2000 for help and get that help in several ways. Here's how to start.

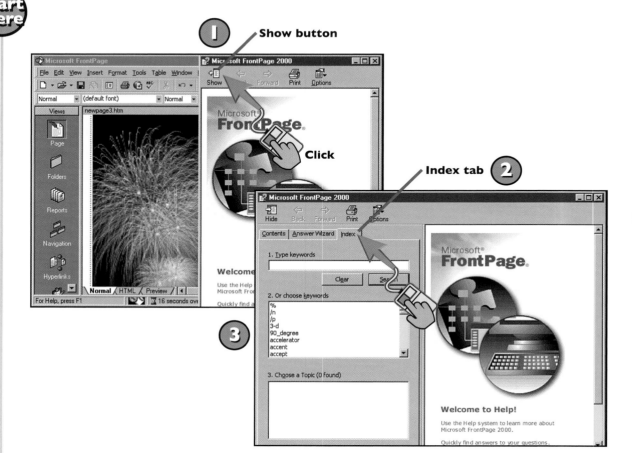

Start Here

Show button

Click

Index tab 2

3

For step 3, you can instead click in the **Type keywords** box and type your best guess for a keyword. If nothing appears in the Choose a Topic box, type a different keyword.

1. Press the **F1** key on your keyboard to open Help. If the whole Help window does not appear, click the **Show** button.

2. Click the **Index** tab.

3. Scroll through the list of keywords under **Or choose keywords**, and click one that appears related to what you want help with.

Next Step

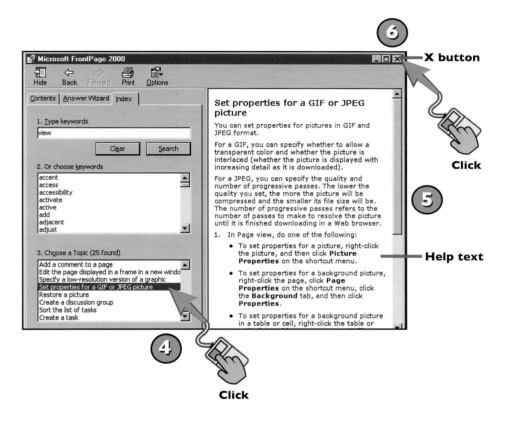

X button

Click

Help text

Click

---

4 Scroll through the list under Choose a Topic, and click the topic that looks like it may hold your answers.

5 Read the Help text displayed in the large box on the right.

6 To close Help, click the **X** button in the upper-right corner of the Help window.

 To print the Help topic you're reading, click the Print button on Help's toolbar.

Task 11: Asking Help to "Answer" a Question

FrontPage Help features an Answer Wizard that can interpret questions you ask in natural language, such as "what is an imagemap?" or "how do I change text color?" I'd recommend giving the index a try first (see Task 10, "Getting Help on a Topic"), but if that's not working for you, see what the Answer Wizard comes up with.

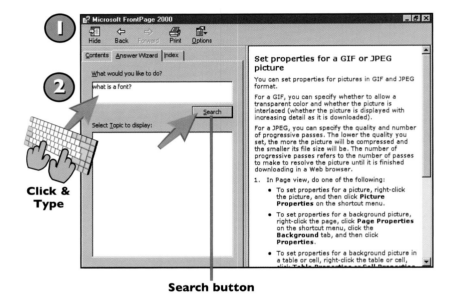

Click & Type

Search button

✓ When phrasing your question, don't worry about capitalization and avoid contractions (type "what is" rather than "what's").

1. Open **Help**, as shown in step 1 of Task 10, then click the **Answer Wizard** tab.

2. Click in the **What would you like to do?** box, type a simple question, and click **Search**.

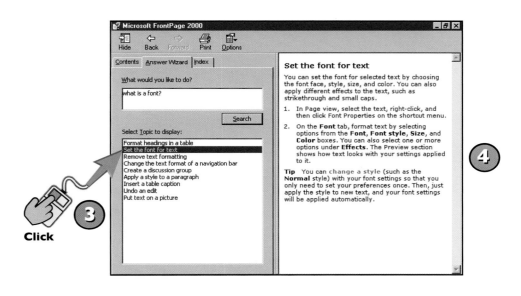

Click

3 Scroll through the list under Select Topic to display, and click one that looks promising.

4 Read the Help text displayed in the large box on the right.

Starting (and Saving) New Web Pages

There's nothing more discouraging than staring at a blank page and knowing you have to find a way to fill it up. You can do that in FrontPage, but you can also take advantage of a variety of tools that take you from blank to beautiful in just a few clicks.

In this part, you'll quickly explore the ins and outs of starting, saving, and viewing your pages, and also begin taking the best shortcuts to terrific pages.

In this part, you'll learn how to get a head start on creating Web pages (and entire Web sites, or **FrontPage Webs**) by basing them on **templates**, predesigned pages you can make into your own by replacing their sample, dummy content with your own words and pictures.

Templates save time, but they present a funny problem for a FrontPage beginner. When you start a page or Web this way, you get a file that contains all sorts of objects (pictures, buttons, links) and formatting (tables, fonts, backgrounds) that you haven't learned to manipulate yet.

It's nothing to worry about. Just keep in mind that when you use a template, you may not understand exactly how to deal with all of your page's predefined objects and formatting until you get farther along in this book.

Tasks

Task 1: Starting Off with a Pre-Started Page

The fastest way to build a great-looking page is to start off with a page in which the design work has already been done for you—a *template*. Then all you'll need to do is to replace the words (and sometimes, the pictures) in the template-based page with your own content. Even though you still have to provide content, a template saves you a ton of time and trouble.

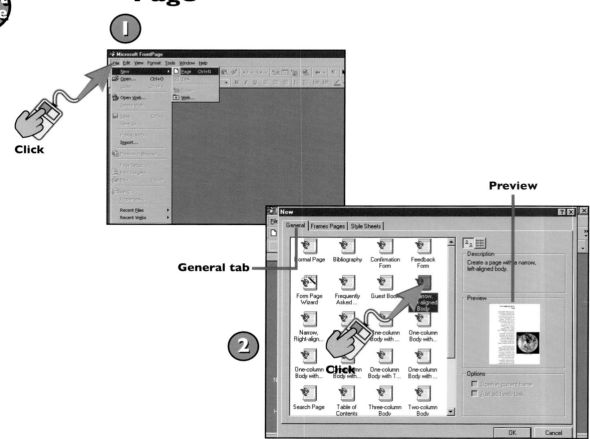

Start Here

Click

Preview

General tab

Click

✓ The introduction to this part includes an important note about using templates. If you skipped it, flip this page to the right and read it now.

✓ Don't worry about making a choice that looks perfectly right—you'll find it's easy to change the style later, especially by changing the *theme* (see Task 6, "Choosing a Theme"). Just look for a page whose overall layout seems right.

1 Click **File**, **New**, and then choose **Page**.

2 One by one, click each of the **icons** in the **General** tab, and watch the Preview to see how a page created with that template will appear.

Next Step

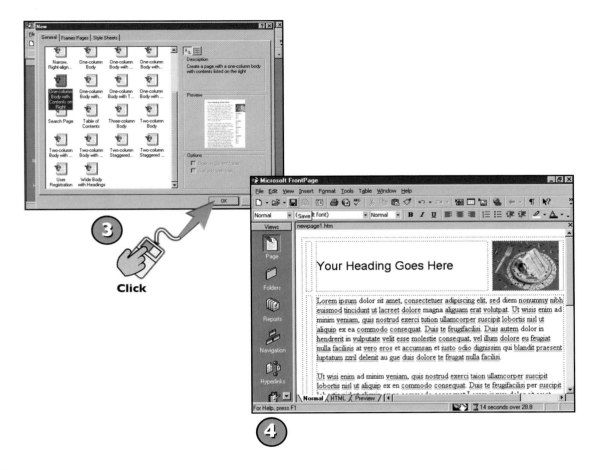

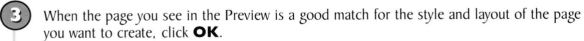

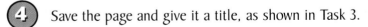

Click

3 When the page you see in the Preview is a good match for the style and layout of the page you want to create, click **OK**.

4 Save the page and give it a title, as shown in Task 3.

✓ After creating the page, you can edit and enhance its content and design any way you want, according to the steps shown throughout the rest of this book. You can even change or remove any of the objects or formatting the template put there—the file is all yours now.

✓ If you feel like creating your page from scratch (and why not?), start off by working with the empty page that appears automatically whenever you open FrontPage from the Start menu. Or just click the **New Page** button on the Standard toolbar.

Task 2: Starting a New Web

In FrontPage-speak, a web is a family of related, interconnected Web pages intended to be explored as a Web site. You'll find it easier for now to deal with creating one page at a time and leave creating whole webs until later ('til Part 9, "Building a Web," to be exact), after you've got the hang of single pages. But just so Webs don't have to remain a complete mystery until then, note that you can start a new Web as easily as a new page.

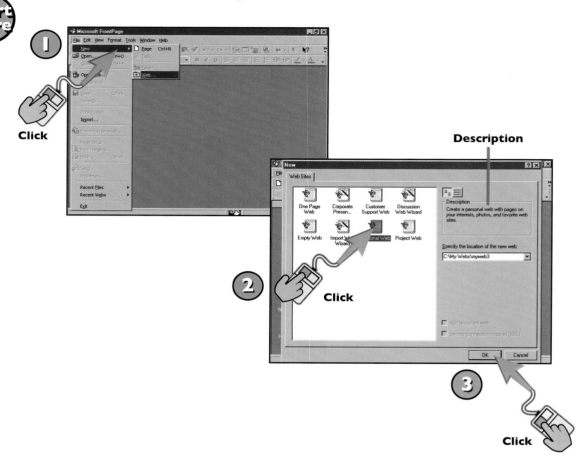

✓ A Web starts out with a default organization and number of pages, but in Part 9 you'll learn how to reorganize a Web and add, delete, and move the pages within it.

1. Click **File**, **New**, and then choose **Web**.

2. Click each of the **icons** in the Web Sites tab, and read the description that appears on the right side of the dialog box.

3. When the description shown is the best available match for the type of site you want to create, click **OK**.

Next Step

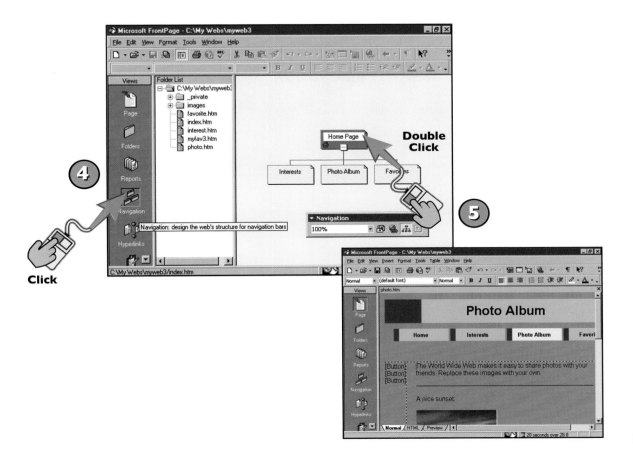

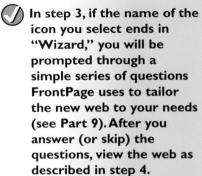

(4) In the Views bar, click the **Navigation** button to switch to Navigation view, which displays a map of the pages in the Web.

(5) To open a page in your web in Page view (so you can edit it), double-click that page in the Navigation map.

In step 3, if the name of the icon you select ends in "Wizard," you will be prompted through a simple series of questions FrontPage uses to tailor the new web to your needs (see Part 9). After you answer (or skip) the questions, view the web as described in step 4.

Task 3: Saving (and Titling) Your Page

When you save your page, you choose not only its filename, but also its *title*. The title of a Web page does not appear within the layout of the page itself, but in the title bar of the browser through which the page is viewed. The title is important because it helps identify your page to Web search tools and in the menus of Bookmarks or Favorites visitors create in their browsers.

Pages in a web created from a template already have titles and filenames, so step 1 alone saves them. See Part 9 to learn how to change the title or filename of a page in a web.

Make your title short but also clear and descriptive. Avoid meaningless, overused titles like "My Home Page," and try to work the most important, identifying keywords into the title.

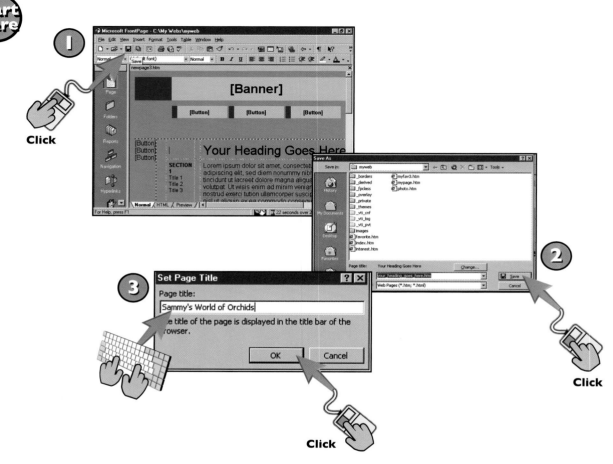

1. While looking at the page in Page view, click the **Save** button on the Standard toolbar.

2. Click the **Change** button.

3. Type a title for this page, and click **OK**.

Save in list

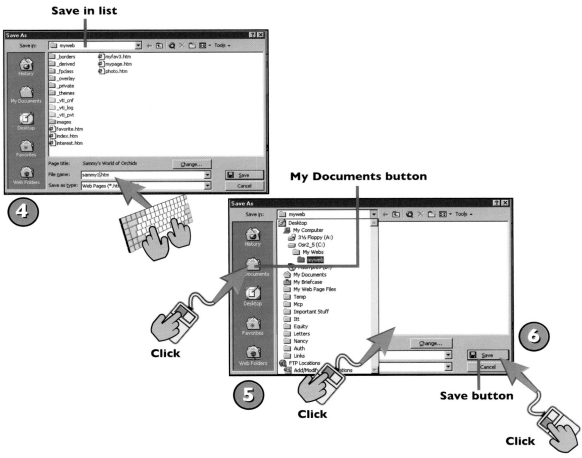

My Documents button

Save button

Click

Click

Click

Click

4 Back on the Save As dialog box, click in the **File name** box, and type a short, descriptive filename.

5 Use the Save In list to choose a folder in which to save this page, or click the **My Documents** button to choose your Windows My Documents folder.

6 Click the **Save** button on the **Save As** dialog box.

✅ When typing a filename in step 4, do not type a filename extension (FrontPage will add .htm for you). Keep the name short and simple, and do not use any punctuation in the filename except dashes (-) or underscores (_).

✅ After the first time you save a file, you'll no longer need to perform steps 2 through 6 when you save again. Step 1 alone saves the file with the title, filename, and folder you've previously selected.

End Task

Task 4: Closing and Re-Opening Pages

As you work on Web pages, you'll probably create them over a series of editing sessions. You'll need to open existing pages and close them when you're done.

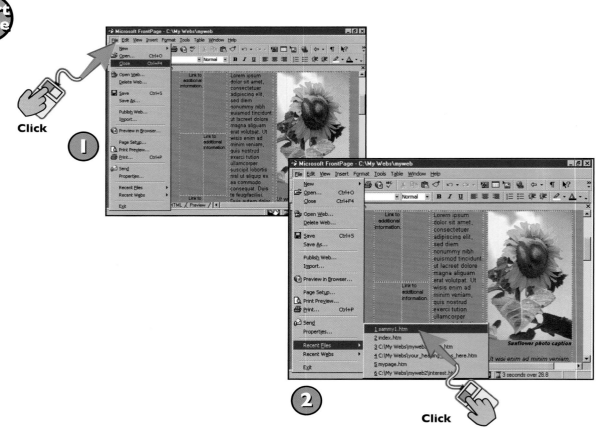

Click

Click

✓ If you open or create a page without first closing another page that's already open, you'll have both pages open at once. That's OK—you can keep two, three, or even more pages open and switch from working on one to any other by choosing a page's name from the Window menu.

1 To close a page file (without closing FrontPage), click **File**, and then choose **Close**.

2 To open one of the page files you've used recently, click **File,** choose **Recent Files**, and then choose the page's filename from the submenu.

Task 5: Opening a Page File You Haven't Used Lately

Open button

If a file you want to work on is not among the files you've edited most recently, its name won't appear on the Recent Files submenu. No problem—here's how to open any page on your PC.

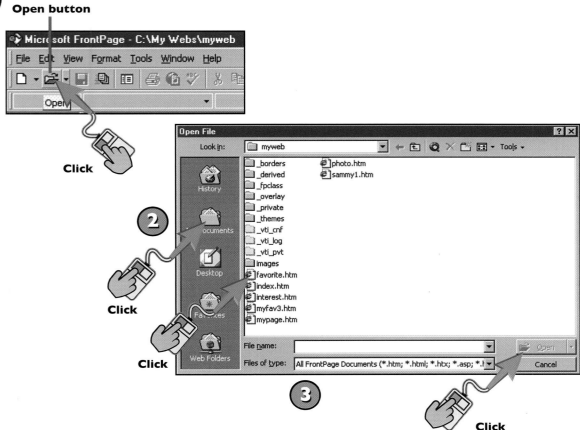

Click

Click

Click

Click

Click

2

3

(1) Click the **Open** button on the Standard toolbar.

(2) Use the Look In list to choose the folder in which the page was last saved, or click the **My Documents** button to look in your My Documents folder.

(3) When you see the page's filename listed among the files and folders shown in the dialog box, click the name and then click the **Open** button on the Open File dialog box.

End Task

Task 6: Choosing a Theme

The visual style of a Web page is determined by a variety of things: the *fonts* (typefaces) and colors used for text, the accent graphics, the background and the style of bullets, among others. A FrontPage theme is a way to choose (or change) all of these at once. Choosing a theme not only saves time, but also helps ensure that all of these visual element choices work well together.

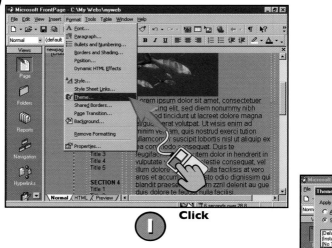

Click

1

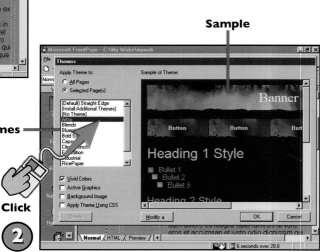

Sample

Themes

Click

2

✓ When previewing the themes, ignore the layout of the page contents shown in the sample. What the theme controls is not the organization of objects on the page, but rather the style of fonts, colors, buttons and so on—so that's what you look at when choosing a theme.

1 While viewing your page in Page view, choose **Format**, and then choose **Theme**.

2 Click **Themes** in the list on the left, watching the **Sample of Theme** to see what a sample page using that theme looks like.

Next Step

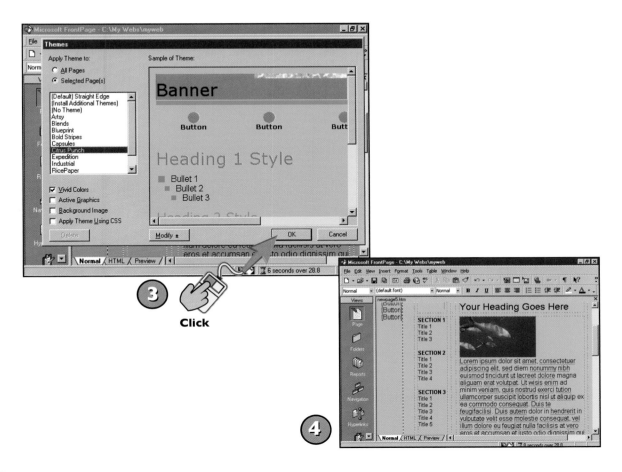

Click

③ When the Sample of Theme shows the fonts, colors, and other stylistic elements that you'd like to use, click **OK**.

④ Continue to add to, edit, and develop your page, and save often.

✓ At any point in the evolution of your page, you can repeat this task and choose a different theme.

✓ If a theme is close to what you want but not quite right, just apply the theme and then change whatever you want to change within the page file itself.

End Task

Task 7: Choosing Which Theme Options to Include

On the Themes dialog box, you'll find a list of four check boxes. Checking each of these check boxes adds some optional formatting. This formatting is optional because it's so advanced that it can be seen only when the page is viewed through the most up-to-date browsers and might not show up in older browsers. You'll learn more about these advanced formatting options later in this book.

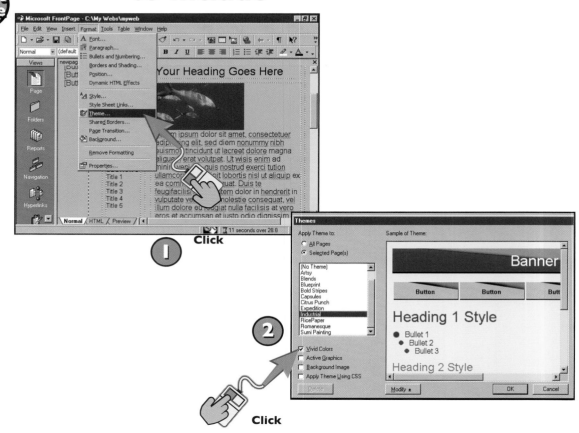

Start Here

Click

1

2

Click

✓ Where no check mark appears, clicking the check box adds a check mark. When a check mark already appears, clicking the check box removes it.

1 While viewing your page in Page view, choose **Format**, and then choose **Theme**.

2 To include extra-cool "vivid" colors, make sure the **Vivid Colors** check box is checked.

Next Step

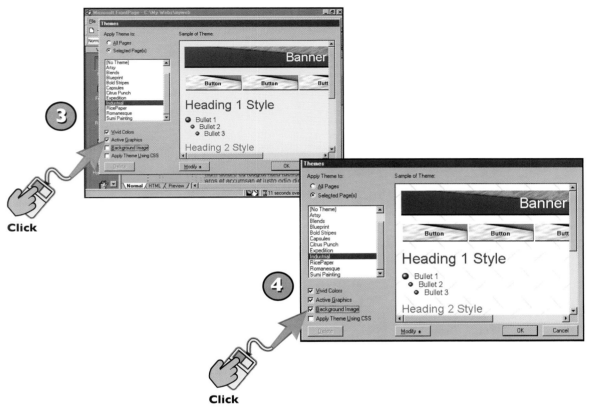

Click

Click

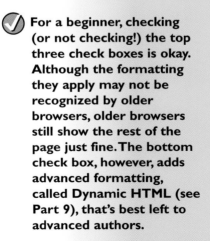

For a beginner, checking (or not checking!) the top three check boxes is okay. Although the formatting they apply may not be recognized by older browsers, older browsers still show the rest of the page just fine. The bottom check box, however, adds advanced formatting, called Dynamic HTML (see Part 9), that's best left to advanced authors.

③ To include animated "Active" buttons and other accent graphics (see Part 9, "Building a Web"), make sure the **Active Graphics** check box is checked.

④ To include a background image (see Part 6, "Adding and Formatting Pictures"), make sure the **Background Image** check box is checked.

Task 8: Previewing Your Page

FrontPage shows your page to you as it will appear online—but not exactly. For example, in **Page** view's **Normal** tab, FrontPage shows you the border lines of tables to help you work with them, even if you've chosen to make those borders invisible online. Some kinds of objects don't do their thing in the **Normal** tab; for example, animations sit still. However, FrontPage offers two "previews" to help you evaluate the way your page will really look to visitors.

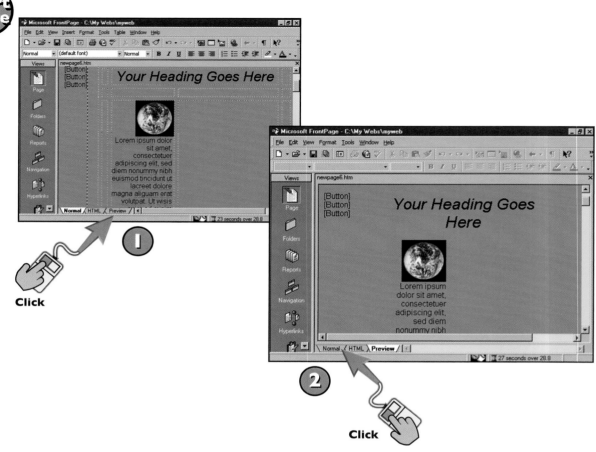

Click

Click

It's impossible to create a page that looks exactly the same no matter which browser it's viewed through. Differences among browsers affect the look of even simple Web pages. Your FrontPage work will look just as you expect in Internet Explorer 4, but may look a little different in other browsers.

1 While viewing (in the Normal tab) the page you want to preview, click the **Preview** tab at the bottom of the FrontPage window.

2 To return to normal Page view, click the **Normal** tab at the bottom of the FrontPage window.

Click

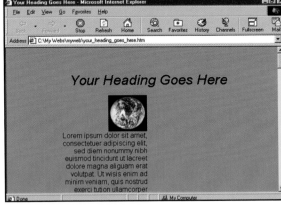

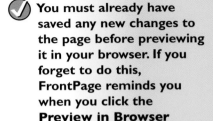

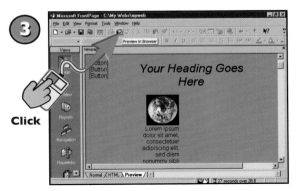
To view the page in the default Web browser on your PC (the one that opens automatically when you start a Web activity from another program), click the **Preview in Browser** button.

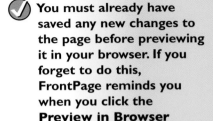
To return to working in FrontPage, close or minimize your browser.

You must already have saved any new changes to the page before previewing it in your browser. If you forget to do this, FrontPage reminds you when you click the **Preview in Browser** button.

End Task

PART 3

Making Pages Say What You Want

Pretty soon, you'll start adding pictures to your page (or replacing pictures the template put there). And by all means, pictures are important. But it's the words, or *text*, that carry most of your content. Text does the critical job of saying what you want your Web page to say. It may not always be the coolest thing on your pages, but it's usually the most important thing.

In this part, you explore the ways you create, edit, and correct Web page text in FrontPage 2000. You'll find that the job is very much like using a word processor—only easier. (And in Part 4, "Saying It with Style," you'll learn how to make that text look sharp!)

Tasks

Task 1: Typing New Text

Got a hole that needs filling with your thoughts? Just type away! As you begin entering text in your Web page, don't worry about what the text looks like. Just get the raw text typed in and deal with how it looks later.

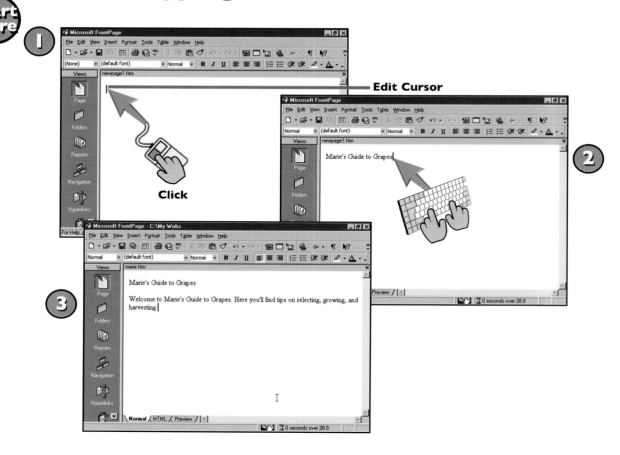

Edit Cursor

Click

✓ When you start with a blank page, the only place you can type new text is at the top of the page. Once text or other objects are in the page, you can insert text in various spots within the page by clicking between objects to position the edit cursor there.

✓ Don't forget to save your Web page file often, especially after adding or changing text.

1 Click the page at the spot where you want to add text. The edit cursor, a flashing vertical bar, appears where you clicked to mark the spot where anything you type will appear.

2 Type your text.

3 When you reach the end of a line, keep typing—the edit cursor jumps automatically to the next line.

Task 2: Starting a New Paragraph

Start Here

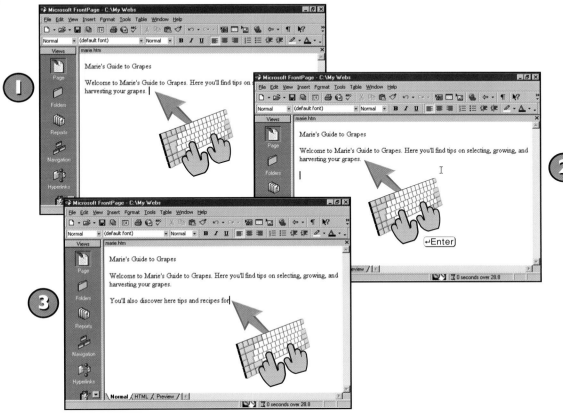

As you'll discover in **Part 4,** *paragraph* has an important and specific meaning in **Web** authoring. Certain types of formatting always apply to a whole paragraph, *never* to only part of a paragraph. So where you choose to break paragraphs—end one and start another—has a big effect on how you can format the text.

✓ To combine two paragraphs into one, put the edit cursor at the very start of the second paragraph, and then press your **Backspace** key.

✓ To see all the *paragraph breaks* (and other invisible formatting marks) in your page, click the **Show All** button on the Standard toolbar while in the Normal tab. The breaks appear as paragraph marks (¶), so you can see where they are, but the marks are never visible online. Click the button again to hide the marks.

① Type to the very end of a paragraph.

② Press your **Enter** key. The edit cursor drops away from the paragraph to a new, blank line.

③ Type the new paragraph.

End Task

Task 3: Typing Symbols and Special Characters

Sometimes you'll need characters that don't appear on your keyboard, such as the copyright symbol or the accented characters used in languages other than English. For such occasions, FrontPage offers its Symbol dialog box.

The codes FrontPage uses for some symbols work great when the page is viewed through a Windows browser, but may not look right when viewed on another computer type (such as a Macintosh). To make your page look great to the non-Windows crowd online, avoid the Symbols dialog box and see a more advanced book to learn to use character codes in *HTML*.

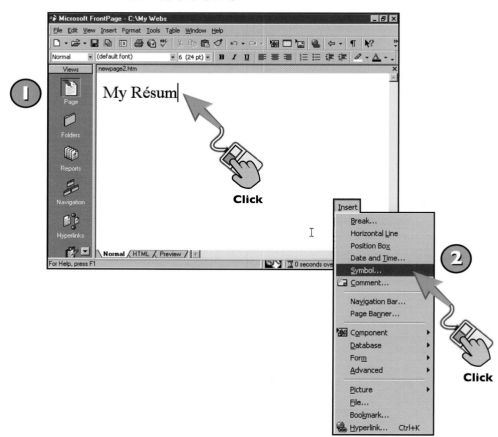

1. Point to the spot in the text where you want to insert the character, and click to position the edit cursor there.

2. Click **Insert**, and then choose **Symbol**.

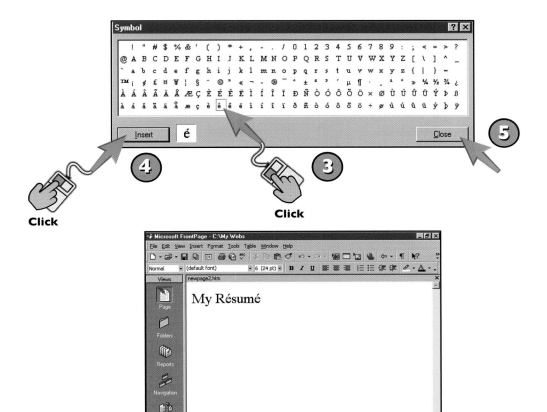

Click

Click

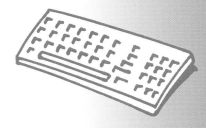

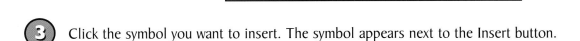

③ Click the symbol you want to insert. The symbol appears next to the Insert button.

④ Click **Insert** to insert the symbol.

⑤ Click **Close**.

✅ You delete a symbol exactly as you would delete any other text (see Task 5).

✅ If you change the font (as you learn to do in Part 4) of text containing symbols, recheck the symbols carefully, and redo them if necessary. Sometimes changing fonts messes up symbols.

End Task

Task 4: Selecting Text

To perform most activities involving text—such as changing the style of text, deleting text, or replacing text with different text—you must first select (highlight) the text you want to work on. You select text in FrontPage in the same way you select text in most other Windows programs.

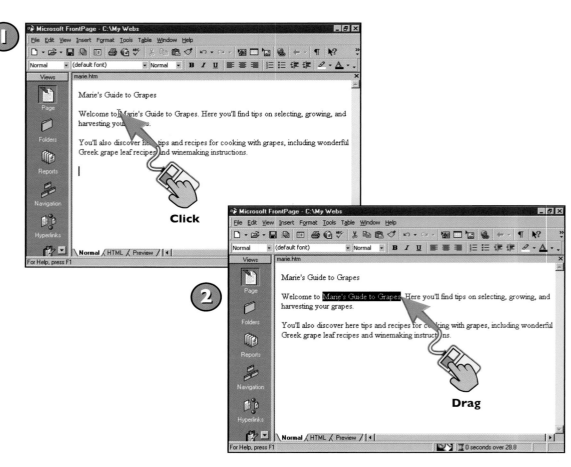

Click

Drag

✓ To deselect text (removing the highlighting), point anywhere in the page and click.

✓ Anything you type automatically replaces any selected text—even if you type only one character, that character replaces all of the selected text. The new text is usually formatted the same way as the text it replaces.

1 Point to the beginning of the text you wish to select.

2 Click and drag to highlight the selection: Drag to the right to select all or part of a line; drag down to select multiple lines.

Task 5: Replacing (or Deleting) Existing Text

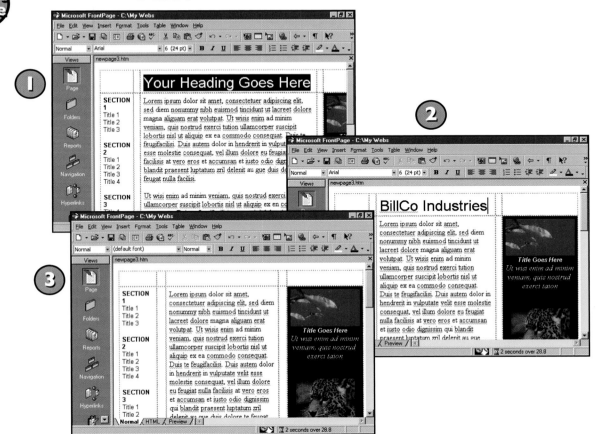

If you started your page with a template (see Part 2, "Starting (and Saving) New Web Pages"), you've got a lot of sample text in your page (mostly in Latin; don't ask me what it means) that you need to replace with your own (or just delete). And even when you don't use a template, replacing and deleting text is an essential page-editing skill—and an easy one.

(1) Select the text you want to change.

(2) To replace the selected text with new text, type your new text.

(3) To delete the selected text, press the **Delete** key on your keyboard.

✓ To replace text with new text that's formatted the same way—same font, size, and so on (see **Part 4**)—replace that text (step 2) rather than deleting it (step 3). If you delete and then type new text, the new text may not show the same formatting as what you deleted.

Task 6: Copying Text

Start Here

If you have a block of text you want to use in more than one place on your page, you needn't type it over and over and over. You can simply type it once and then copy it wherever you need it.

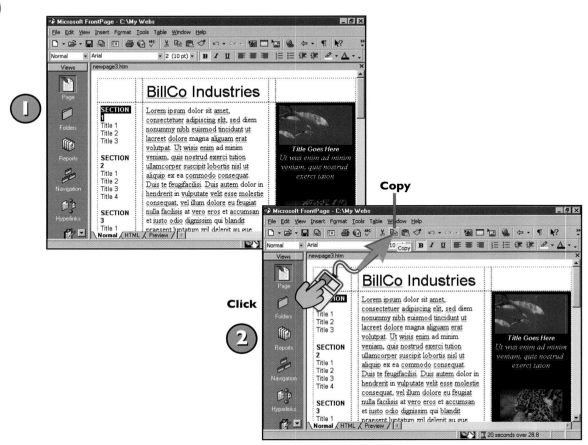

Copy

Click

To copy text from another Windows program—such as your word processor—to a page, perform steps 1 and 2 in the other program, switch to FrontPage, and perform steps 3 and 4 in the page file in FrontPage.

① Select the text you want to copy.

② Click the **Copy** button on the Standard toolbar.

Next Step

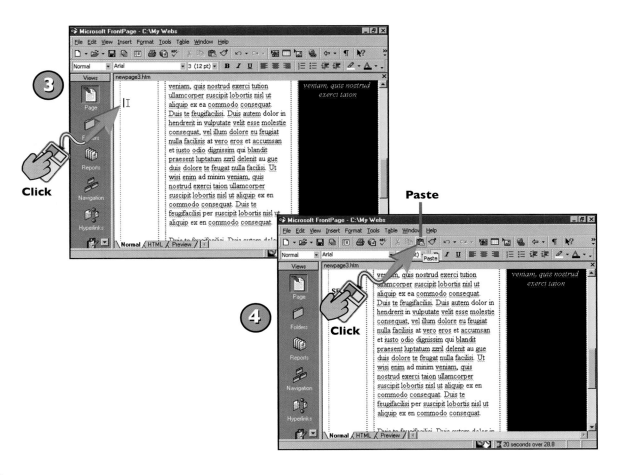

Paste

Click

Click

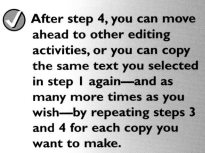

③ Point to the spot where you want to copy the text and click to position the edit cursor there.

④ Click the **Paste** button on the Standard toolbar.

After step 4, you can move ahead to other editing activities, or you can copy the same text you selected in step I again—and as many more times as you wish—by repeating steps 3 and 4 for each copy you want to make.

End Task

Task 7: Moving Text

Moving text is really just like copying—except that you don't leave the original text behind. You *cut* it from one place and then *paste* it in another.

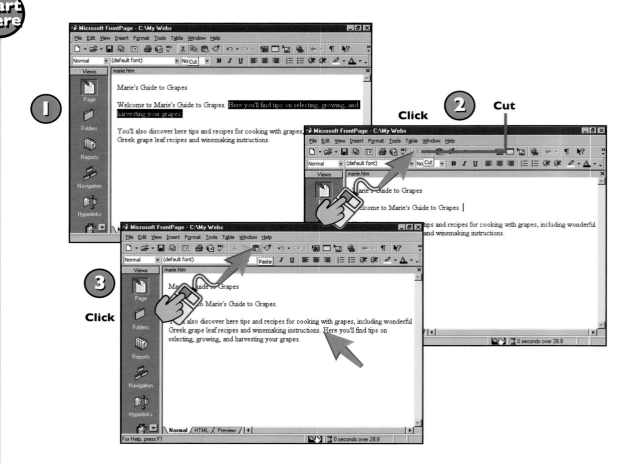

✅ Don't try to use your Delete key instead of the Cut button in step 2— Delete removes the text just like Cut, but doesn't remember the text so it can be copied in step 3.

✅ Just as when you're copying, after moving, you can paste as many copies as you wish of the text you cut in step 2. Just repeat step 3 for each copy you need.

1 Select the text you want to move.

2 Click the **Cut** button on the Standard toolbar.

3 Click in the spot where you want to move the text, and then click **Paste**.

Task 8: Checking Spelling as You Go Along

Start Here

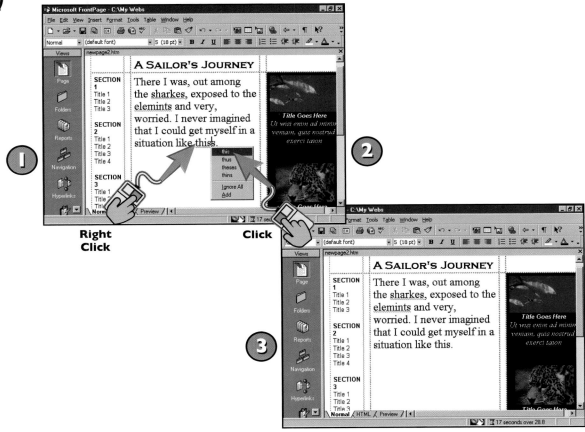

Right Click

Click

While typing in the Normal tab, you may have noticed a zigzag red underline under some words. That's the automatic spell-checker at work—it zigzag underlines any word it doesn't recognize, to alert you to check that word. You can simply fix the word when it's really misspelled or ignore the underlines (they don't show up online) when you disagree with the spell-checker. But there's more you can do.

✓ The spell-checker marks all words it doesn't recognize—the words may be misspelled, but they may just be names or other words that aren't in FrontPage's dictionary. To add an often used word (such as your name) to the dictionary so that the checker knows it's not an error, right-click the underlined word and then choose **Add**.

1 Right-click the underlined word.

2 Read any suggestions offered in bold atop the menu, and if one is correct, click it to replace your word with the suggestion.

3 If your original word is actually correct, click **Ignore All** to prevent that word from being marked as an error in this page.

End Task

Task 9: Running the Spell-Checker, On Demand

Despite the as-you-go spell-checker (see Task 8), it's smart to run FrontPage's on-demand spell-checker, too. I'm a born proofreader, but you'd be amazed at the mistakes Que's editors rescue me from!

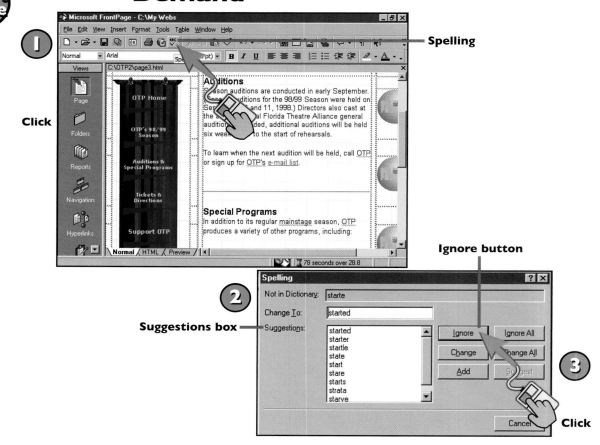

Spelling

Click

Ignore button

Suggestions box

Click

✓ If a page has no misspellings, the box for step 6 appears immediately after step 1.

✓ When performing step 3, you can click **Ignore All** to make the spell-checker automatically ignore that word everywhere it finds it in this spell-check run.

✓ To add an often used word (such as your name) to the dictionary so that the checker knows it's not an error, click the **Add** button the next time the checker stops on that word.

1 Click the **Spelling** button on the Standard toolbar. The Spelling dialog box shows the first unrecognized word found in the page.

2 Read the word shown in Not in Dictionary (that's what you typed), and examine the suggested alternative spellings listed in the Suggestions box.

3 If the word is correctly spelled in the Not in Dictionary box, click **Ignore**.

Change button

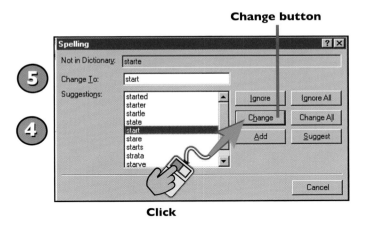

Click

⑤

④

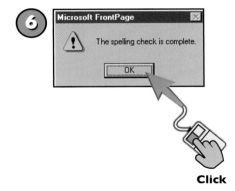

Click

⑥

④ If the word is misspelled but one suggestion is correct, click the suggested word and then click **Change**.

⑤ If the word is misspelled and no correct suggestion appears, fix the word in the **Change To** box, and then click **Change**.

⑥ After you perform step 3, 4 or 5, the spell-checker moves ahead to the next unrecognized word. When you have dealt with all unrecognized words, the checker reports that it's finished.

Task 10: Looking Up Synonyms

If a word you typed seems sort of right for your intended meaning—but not *just* right—FrontPage's built-in thesaurus can suggest some alternative words with the same meaning—*synonyms*. One of those synonyms may be exactly the word that works. And if not, hey— you're no worse off, right?

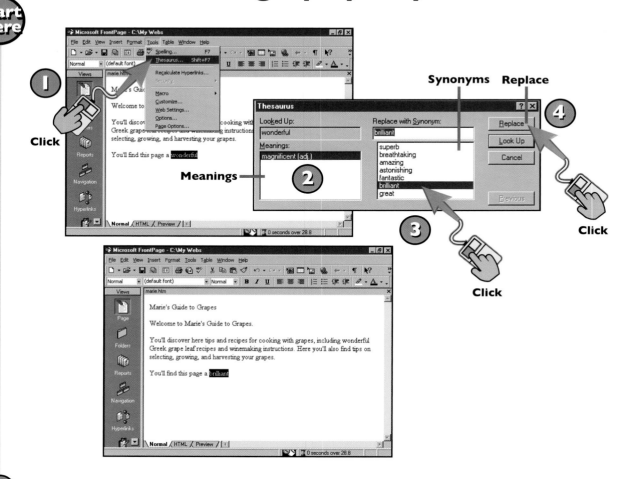

✓ If you don't like any of the suggested synonyms better than your original word, click **Cancel** in the Thesaurus dialog box.

✓ To display a new list of synonyms based on one of the suggestions, click the suggestion and then click the **Look Up** button.

1 Select the word you want to see synonyms for, choose **Tools**, and then choose **Thesaurus**.

2 If there are two or more choices in the Meanings box, pick the one that most closely matches the meaning you want.

3 In the list of synonyms on the right, click the word you want to use.

4 Click **Replace** to close the thesaurus and replace your original word with the synonym.

Task 11: Finding Text

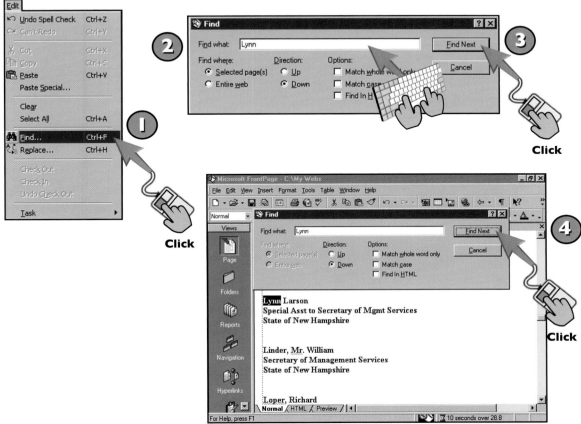

In a very long page or web, you may have trouble quickly locating specific words or passages you want to edit or review. That's when FrontPage's Find feature does its thing.

Click

Click

Click

To find only instances of the Find What text that match the exact capitalization you typed, click the **Match case** check box to put a check mark there.

In the Find dialog box, observe the Entire Web option offered under Find Where. When you create webs (see Part 9), you can use this option to search a whole Web for the Find What text.

1. Click at the very top of the page, choose **Edit**, and then choose **Find**.

2. In the Find what box, type the word or phrase you want to locate.

3. Click **Find Next**. FrontPage scrolls to the first instance of the Find What text in the page and highlights it.

4. If the instance is the one you wanted to work on, click **Cancel**. If not, click **Find Next** again to move to the next instance.

Task 12: Making "Global" Text Changes

If you've done much editing in a word processor, you know about global changes, sometimes called "find & replace." In a global change, you change a word or phrase to something else, not just in one place but anywhere and everywhere in the page that it appears, all at once. It's a great time saver.

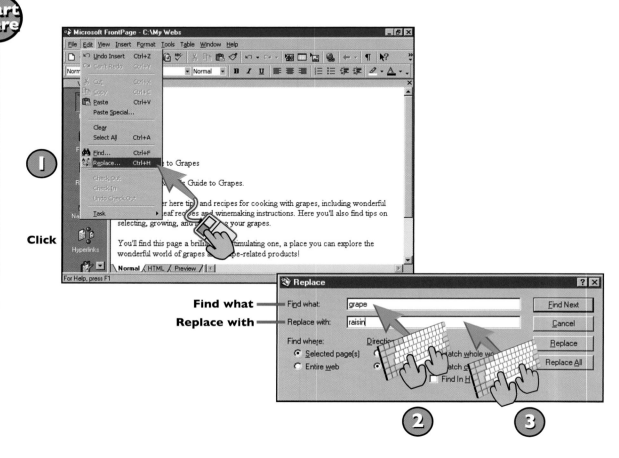

Find what

Replace with

To change only instances of the Find What text that match the exact capitalization you typed in Find What, click the **Match case** check box to put a check mark there.

1. Click at the very top of the page, and choose **Edit, Replace** from the menu bar.

2. In the Find What box, type the word or phrase you want to change.

3. In the Replace With box, type what you want the text from step 2 changed to.

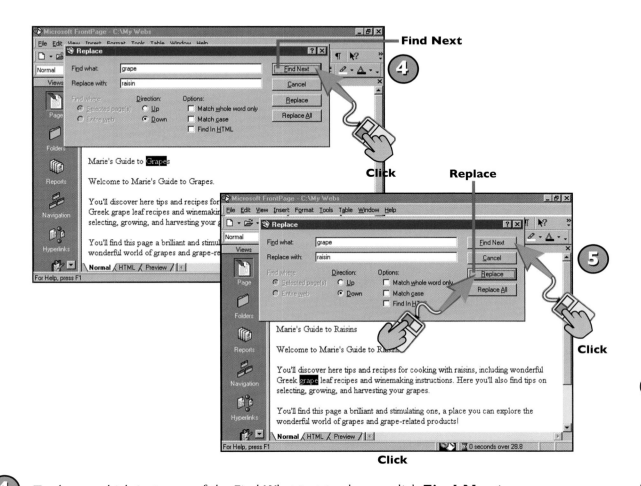

Find Next

Click

Replace

Click

Click

④ To choose which instances of the Find What text to change, click **Find Next**.

⑤ Each time the checker stops on an instance of the Find What text, click **Replace** to replace it or **Find Next** to leave it alone and find the next instance.

✓ To change all instances of the Find What text to the Replace With text without checking each, click **Replace All**.

✓ In the Replace dialog box, observe the Entire Web option offered under Find Where. When you create webs (see Part 9), you can use this option to replace all instances of Find What in all pages of the web.

Saying It with Style

Depending on how you approach your page, you may need all—or none—of the text formatting techniques in this part.

If you begin with a template and just replace the text that's there, the text is preformatted, and you can leave the formatting alone if you're happy with it. And if you choose a theme, you'll find that you can do most or all of your text formatting simply by selecting a **style** (see Task 1) for each paragraph.

But as your confidence grows, you'll probably want ever-increasing control of text formatting, so you can tune and tailor the look of your text to your precise requirements. In this part, you'll explore all of the ways you can change the look of text—from the simple to the sublime.

Tasks

Task 1: Choosing the Style of a Paragraph

The most important step in controlling the appearance of text is choosing the text's *paragraph style* from the Style list. There are many styles, but the most important are the six different Heading styles (from big Heading 1 to little Heading 6), Normal style (for ordinary paragraphs), and the List styles (see Task 11). But feel free to experiment with all of the styles.

✓ To apply a style to multiple, consecutive paragraphs all at once, click anywhere in the first paragraph and drag down through the paragraphs to anywhere in the last paragraph. Then choose your style.

✓ The exact formatting applied by a style (and the particular list of styles available) depends on the theme you have chosen. If the page does not use a theme, the styles apply simple default formatting.

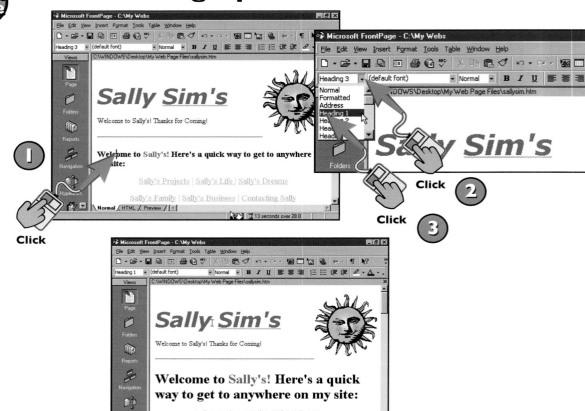

1 Click anywhere within the paragraph you want to format. (You do not need to select the paragraph.)

2 Click the **down arrow** on the right end of the Style box to open the Style list.

3 Click the name of the style you wish to apply.

Task 2: Indenting a Paragraph

Start Here

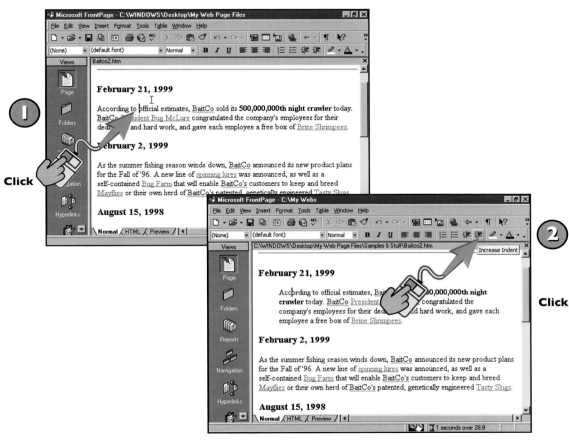

Click

Click

To indent text is to push it inward from the margin to make it stand out on the page and to better show that the indented text is a part of the heading or other text above it. Indenting selected paragraphs can give your page structure and visual variety.

1 Click anywhere within the paragraph you want to indent. (You do not need to select the paragraph.)

2 Click the **Increase Indent** button on the Formatting toolbar. (To indent farther, click the **Increase Indent** button multiple times.)

✓ To indent multiple, consecutive paragraphs at once, click anywhere in the first paragraph and drag down through the paragraphs to anywhere in the last paragraph. Then click **Increase Indent**.

✓ To remove the indent, repeat step 1, and then click the **Decrease Indent** button on the Formatting toolbar.

End Task

Task 3: Lining Up Paragraphs on the Left, Right, or in the Center

You can align any paragraph in any of three different ways: tight up against the left side of the page (left alignment), centered on the page (center alignment), or hard up to the right side (right alignment).

✓ To align multiple, consecutive paragraphs, click anywhere in the first paragraph and drag down through the paragraphs to anywhere in the last paragraph. Then click the alignment button you want.

✓ Most of the time, left alignment is best, especially for Normal-style paragraphs. Center can be nice for large headings (such as Heading 1 or Heading 2 style), especially if not used too much. Save right alignment for special needs.

Start Here

Click

Click

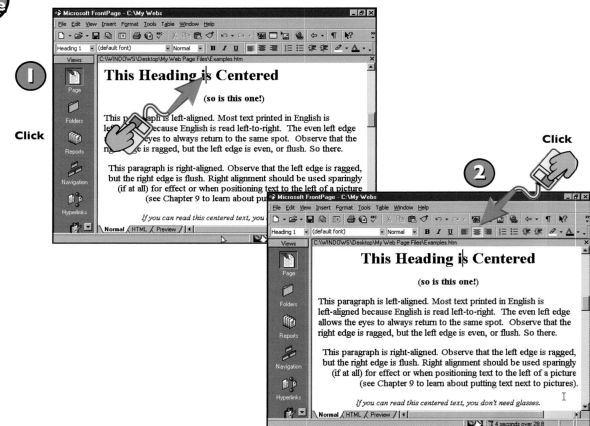

① Click anywhere within the paragraph you want to align. (You do not need to select the paragraph.)

② Click one of the three alignment buttons on the Formatting toolbar: **Align Left**, **Center**, or **Align Right**.

End Task

Task 4: Making Text Bold, Italic, or Underlined

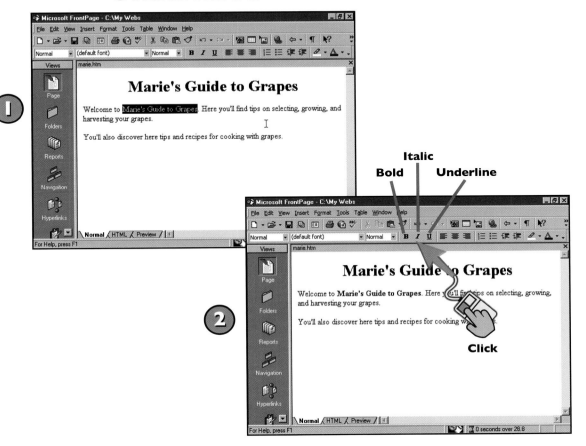

Italic

Bold   **Underline**

Click

Just as in any letter or report you might create, **bold**, *italic*, and <u>underlining</u> are valuable tools in a Web page for making text stand out or for making it match editorial standards (such as setting book titles in italics). They're easy to use, but use them sparingly; too much of this stuff makes text busy and hard to read.

①　Select the exact characters you want to format.

②　Click a button to format the selected characters: the **Bold** button, **Italic** button, or **Underline** button.

✓ To remove bold, italic, or underlining, select the text and click the button again. For example, to de-bold some bold text, select it and click the **Bold** button.

✓ You can combine these kinds of formatting; for example, you can make the selected text both bold and italic by clicking the **Bold** button and then the **Italic** button.

Task 5: Choosing a Font for Text

The best way to control the appearance of text is to choose an appropriate style (see Task 1), especially if you use a theme. But beyond the styles, you can dress up text even more by choosing a particular typeface—or *font*—for it, just as you might choose fonts in a word processor.

✓ Fonts are a form of character formatting, not paragraph formatting, so they affect only the exact characters you select. To apply a font to a whole paragraph, you must select the whole paragraph. The same is true of other character formatting, such as size, bold, italic, underlining, and color (see Tasks 4, 6, 7, and 8).

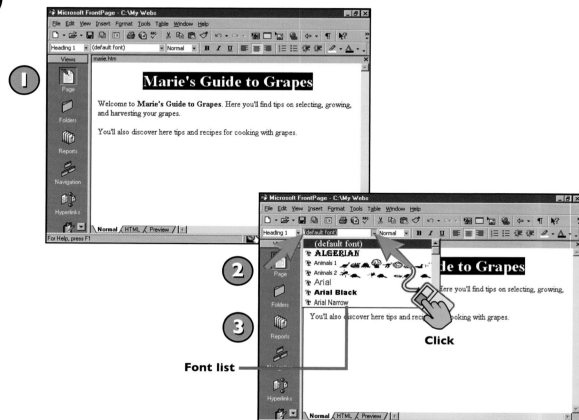

Font list

Click

1. Select the exact characters you want to apply a new font to, so that they're highlighted.

2. Locate the Font list box in the Formatting toolbar. (Observe that the box tells the name of the font that's now applied to the text you selected.)

3. Click the arrow on the right side of the list box to open the list.

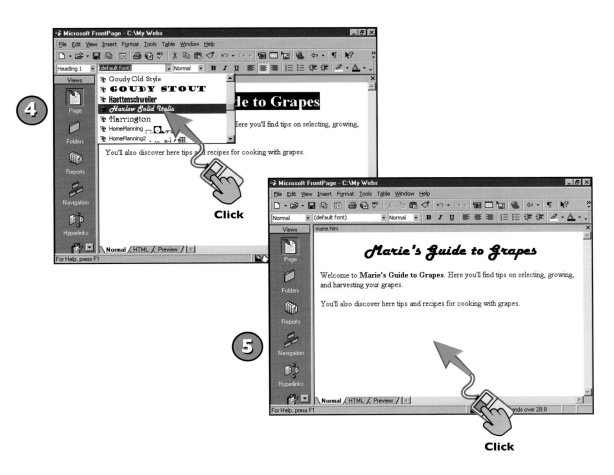

4 Click the font you want to apply.

5 Click anywhere in your page to deselect the text.

 Some browsers (especially unusual or older ones) don't support fonts. If you've used fonts, visitors using those browsers will still see your text, but they won't see it styled exactly the way you intend.

Task 6: Making Text Bigger or Smaller

The paragraph style you choose automatically determines the size of the text. For example, if text set in Heading 3 style looks too small to you, the best solution is to change it to a bigger style, such as Heading 2 or Heading 1. Still, you can fine-tune the size of selected text easily when the size chosen by the style isn't exactly what you want.

In the Font Size list, next to each size there's a point size (8 pt. and so on). In publishing, points measure the height of capital letters (72 pt. = 1 inch). The points are shown to help you estimate the size, but they're not meaningful, because the exact size of text depends upon the screen dimensions of the computer monitor on which it is viewed.

Font Size

Click

1. Select the exact characters you want to make bigger or smaller.

2. Click the arrow at the right end of the **Font Size** box to open the list.

3. Choose a size, from 1 (smallest) to 36 (largest). (Choose **Normal** to allow the applied paragraph style to determine the font size.)

Task 7: Choosing the Color of Text

Start Here

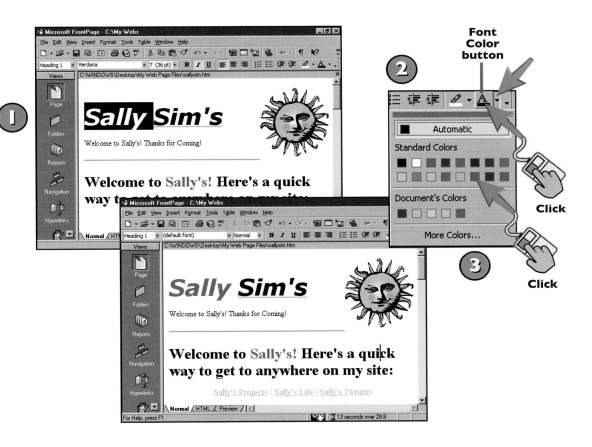

Font Color button

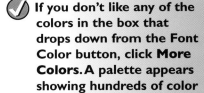

Click

Click

If you choose a theme or start your page with a template (see Part 2), text colors have already been selected to go together well with one another and to contrast properly with any colored background. When you apply styles, they apply color for you, too. So you may never need to choose text colors. Still, you may find yourself wanting to give a heading or other selected text its own unique color. Here's how.

1. Select the exact characters you want to choose a color for.

2. If the color shown in the **Font Color** button is what you want, click the button. If you want a different color, click the tiny arrow on the right side of the **Font Color** button.

3. Click the colored square containing the color you wish to apply. (To allow the paragraph style to determine the color, click **Automatic**.)

✓ If you don't like any of the colors in the box that drops down from the Font Color button, click **More Colors**. A palette appears showing hundreds of color choices. Click a color, and then click **OK**.

Task 8: Giving Text a "Highlight" Color

A highlight color lays a bar of transparent color over selected text, creating the same kind of effect you get when you mark printed text with a highlight marker. Used sparingly, a highlight color is a fun and effective way to make text stand out.

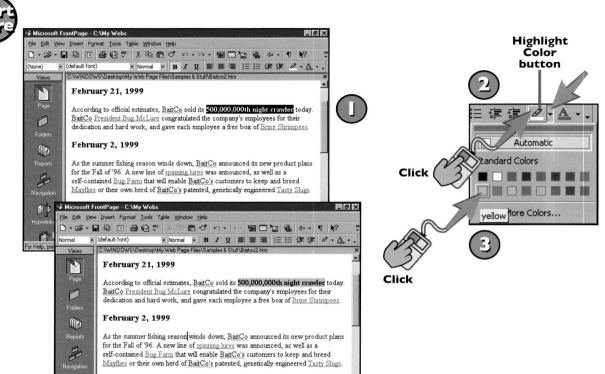

✓ When choosing font colors, highlight colors, and a background (see Part 6, "Adding and Formatting Pictures"), be careful that all of the colors contrast well enough to make the text readable.

✓ If you don't like any of the colors in the box that drops down from the Highlight Color button, click **More Colors**. A palette appears showing hundreds of color choices.

① Select the exact characters you want to highlight.

② If the color shown in the **Highlight Color** button is what you want, click the button. If you want a different color, click the tiny arrow on the right side of **Highlight Color** button.

③ Click the colored square containing the color you want to apply. (To allow the paragraph style to determine the color, click **Automatic**.)

Task 9: "Painting" the Formatting

Start Here

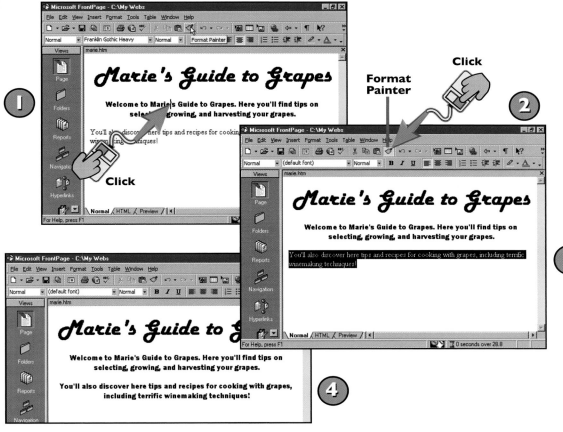

Suppose you have two paragraphs that are formatted differently, and you want them to be formatted the same. FrontPage features a Format Painter that lets you easily copy all paragraph formatting (style, alignment, indent) and character formatting (font, size, color, bold, and so on) from one paragraph to another, so the two paragraphs are formatted identically.

(1) Click in the paragraph whose formatting you want to copy.

(2) Click the **Format Painter** button on the Standard toolbar. (When you move your pointer onto the work area of the page, it becomes a paintbrush to show that Format Painter is active.)

(3) Select the entire paragraph to which you want to apply the formatting.

(4) Click anywhere to de-select the paragraph.

✓ To copy just some character formatting (without any paragraph formatting), select some text formatted the way you like (but not a whole paragraph), click the **Format Painter,** and then select the exact characters to which you want the character formatting applied.

End Task

Task 10: Finding the Super-Formatting Options

As a rule, you should stick with the kinds of character formatting discussed in Tasks 4 through 8. The use of most other, more advanced formatting options can make your page too busy and hard to read, and they're not supported in some browsers. But just in case you feel ambitious, here's how to apply a variety of different advanced formatting options.

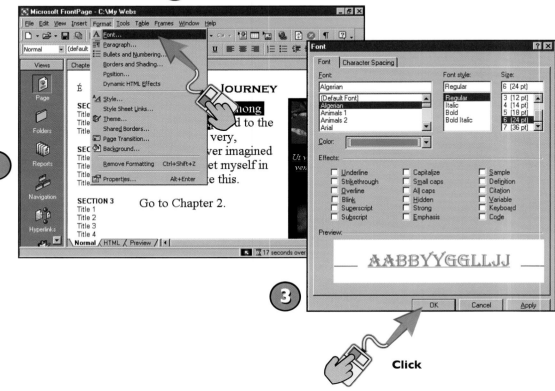

2 Click

3 Click

To change the spacing between characters in selected text (spreading out characters or cramming them more closely together), do steps 1 and 2, and then choose the **Character Spacing** tab and select from the options offered there.

1 Select the exact characters you want to format.

2 Choose **Format,** and then **Font**.

3 Choose from the lists and check the check boxes on the **Font** tab. When the Preview shows the formatting you want, click **OK**.

Start Here

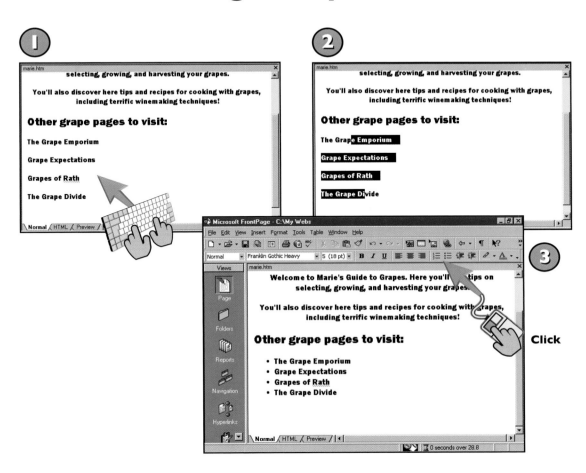

Lists come in two types: In a *numbered list*, the items in the list are preceded by consecutive numbers, and in a *bulleted list*, each item in the list is preceded by a symbol, a "bullet" character, to give the list a little jazz. Lists are a great way to organize content while at the same time giving your page more style.

Click

✓ List formatting is paragraph formatting, so you can select a list by running a selection from anywhere in the top item to anywhere in the bottom item. **Don't worry if part of the top item and part of the bottom item aren't selected.**

① Type the list items, pressing **Enter** after each so that each list item is on a separate line.

② Select the entire list by clicking anywhere in the top item, holding down the mouse button, and dragging to anywhere in the last.

③ Click one of the two list buttons on the Formatting toolbar: **Numbering** or **Bullets**.

✓ When the order of the items in the list is important, as in step-by-step instructions, use a numbered list. When the order doesn't matter, use a bulleted list.

End Task

Task 12: Changing the Bullet or Numbering Style of a List

You can make a pretty good-looking list just by clicking a button, as you did in the previous task. But you don't have to settle for what you get. You can easily modify the appearance of a list, choosing the numbering style (A, B, C; I, II, III; and so on) or bullet symbol.

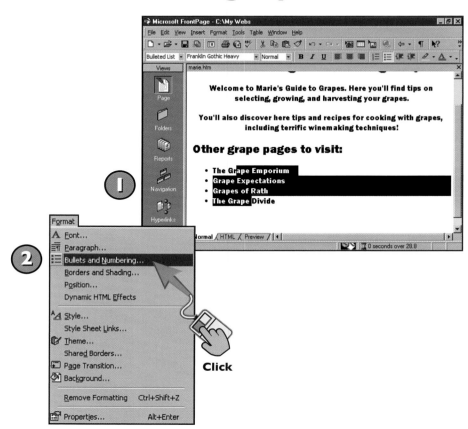

If your page has a theme, the theme may put cool, graphical bullets on your bulleted lists. You can use this task to switch from the graphical bullets to any style on the **Plain Bullets** box. To restore the graphical bullets later, repeat steps 1 and 2, and then click the **Use images from current theme** option on the Image Bullets tab.

1 Select the list by clicking anywhere in the top item, holding down the mouse button, and dragging to anywhere in the last.

2 Click **Format**, and then choose **Bullets and Numbering**.

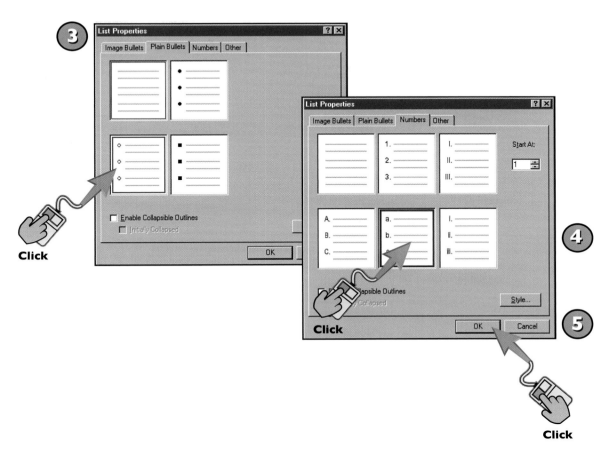

Click

Click

Click

③ To choose a bullet style, click the **Plain Bullets** tab, and click the box showing the type of bullets you want.

④ To choose a number (or consecutive letters) style, click the **Numbers** tab, and click the box showing the type of numbering you want.

⑤ Click **OK** to close the List Properties dialog box.

✓ **On the Other tab of the List Properties dialog box, you can choose from a few kinds of lists other than bulleted and numbered. These aren't used often, so I won't show them here—but if you're curious, try 'em out.**

Task 13: Nesting Items in a List

A complex, or *nested*, list contains some items indented under others. This book's Table of Contents is an example; the tasks are nested beneath each part heading. You can create such lists, going several levels deep and even changing the bullet or number style for nested objects to help them stand out.

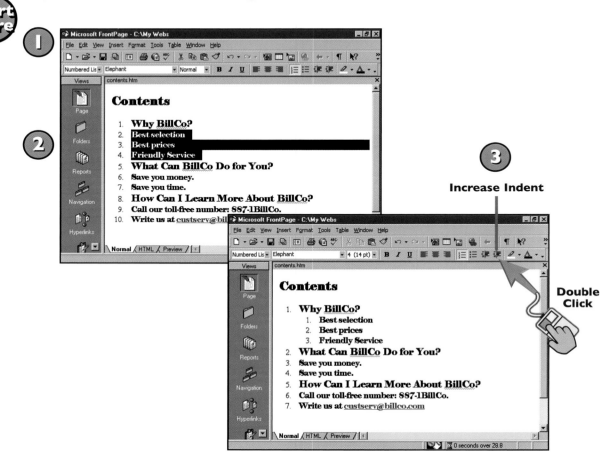

Increase Indent

Double Click

✓ Always click **Increase Indent** *twice* to nest list items.

✓ Beside varying the number style for each level in a numbered list, you can also dress up a bulleted list by varying the bullet style with each level.

1 Create the list as a simple, unnested list, as in Task 11. (Do not indent any items yet.)

2 Select a group of items to be nested.

3 Click the **Increase Indent** button on the Formatting toolbar twice.

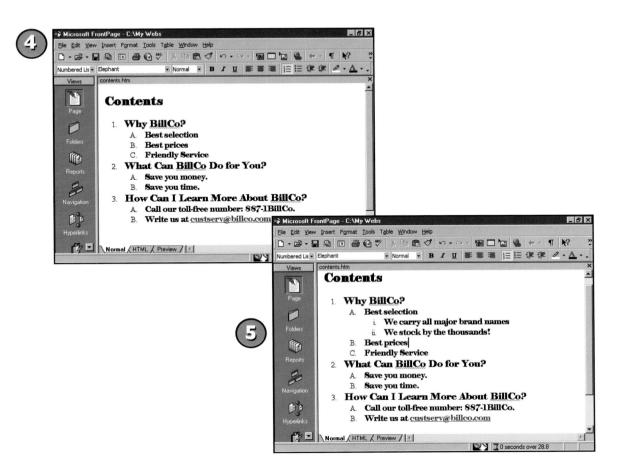

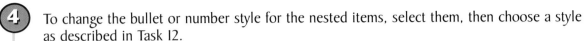

4 To change the bullet or number style for the nested items, select them, then choose a style as described in Task 12.

5 To create each deeper level of nesting, select only the items to be moved to the next level, and click **Increase Indent** twice.

In a numbered list, the numbers in each nested portion are numbered independently, starting at 1 (or a, or I, and so on). That's the way outlines and other nested lists are usually structured. But if you want to change where the numbering begins in any part of the list, select that part, choose **Format, Bullets and Numbering**, and then choose your desired starting number under **Start At**.

Task 14: Creating a Collapsible List

A really long, complicated list is a problem in a Web page; it forces the visitor to scroll too much, and it makes finding any major heading in the list difficult because of all the intervening nested detail. The answer is a *collapsible list*, a nested list in which only top-level items show— at first. When the visitor clicks any top-level item, all nested items beneath it appear.

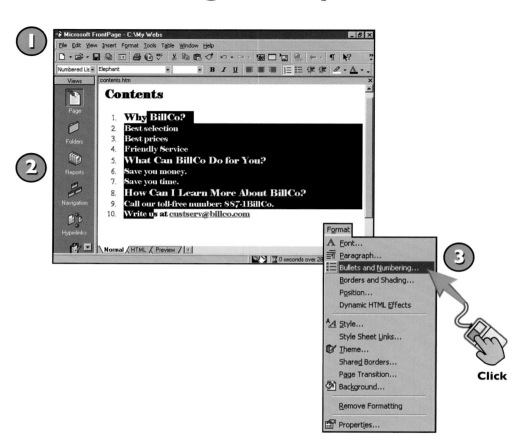

✓ Some folks on the Web need a little coaching on collapsible lists. Near the list, it's usually a good idea to add "Click any item to see more detailed choices," or words to that effect.

① Create a simple list, as described in Task 11. (Don't nest anything yet.)

② Select the list by clicking in the top item, holding down the mouse button, and dragging to anywhere in the last item.

③ Click **Format**, and then choose **Bullets and Numbering**.

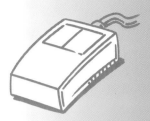

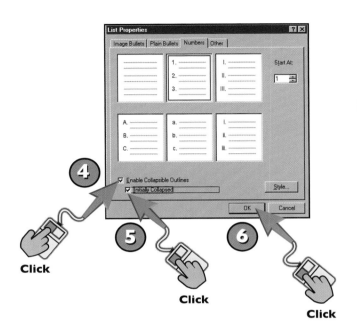

 4

Click

5 **Click**

6 **Click**

 7

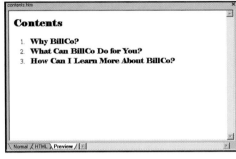

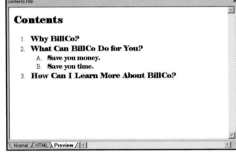

4 Click the box labeled **Enable Collapsible Outlines** to place a check mark there.

5 Click the box labeled **Initially Collapsed**, so the nested items will be hidden when the visitor arrives at the page.

6 Click **OK** to close the List Properties dialog box.

7 Nest items as described in Task 13.

✓ The collapsing effect of a collapsed list does not show up in the **Normal tab** of FrontPage's Page view. To see your list do its thing, save your page, and then click the **Preview tab** or preview the page in your browser. Clicking a list item displays items nested beneath it; clicking it again hides them.

 End Task

Making Hyperlinks

You know links: They're the things you can click in a Web page that take you somewhere else (or do other stuff, such as start a file download).

Although in some ways links may seem like one of the more technical aspects of a Web page, they're surprisingly easy to create in FrontPage 2000. The only tricky part is deciding where you want a link to lead; the rest is a piece o' cake.

In this part, you'll learn what links are, how they work, and how to link from your pages to other pages on the Internet, to files, and to email addresses. You'll also learn the basics of linking from one of your own pages to another of your own pages—the kind of linking that forms a multi-page Web site.

However, keep in mind that when you create and manage a FrontPage web, you gain access to an array of tools for easily linking among all the pages in your web. You'll learn about those in Part 9, "Building a Web."

Tasks

Task 1: Exploring How Links Work

Every link has two parts: the *link source*—the text, picture, or button that a visitor clicks to activate the link—and the *URL*—the address of the page to which that link takes the visitor. Creating links is really just a matter of creating the link source in your page, and then adding the URL behind it.

You can learn a lot more about links by studying the link sources and URLs in the pages you visit online.

When the link source is text, it usually appears underlined and in a unique color. When the link source is a picture, you can locate the link by pointing to the picture; if it's a link, the pointer becomes a pointing hand.

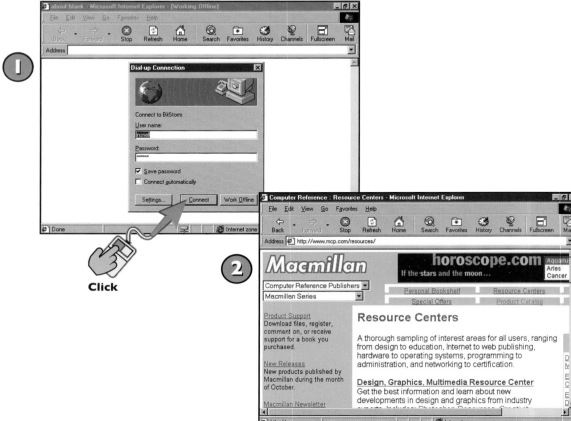

Click

1 Open your Web browser and connect to the Internet.

2 Surf to a page you like that contains links.

Next Step

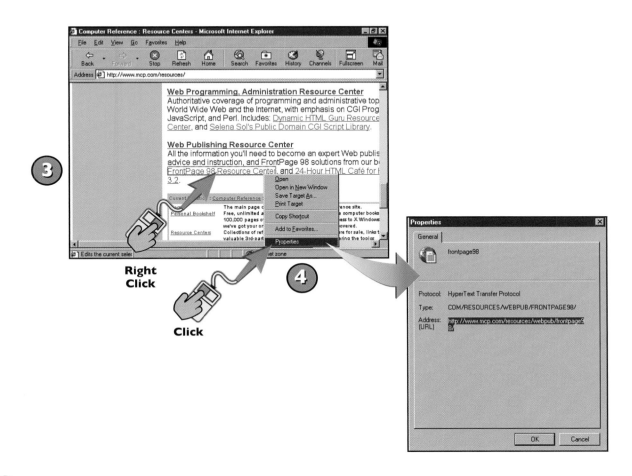

Right Click

Click

Point to a link whose link source is text and right-click it.

Click **Properties**. The Properties dialog box reports the address (URL) to which the link points, along with other information.

✓ You can copy a Web page address from the Properties dialog box by dragging to select the address, right-clicking it, and choosing **Copy**. If you then go immediately to FrontPage to create a link in a page, you can paste the URL into the Create Hyperlink dialog box by clicking there and pressing **Ctrl-V** or **Shift+Ins**.

Task 2: Creating Links to Other People's Web Pages

Now that you grasp the basics of what a link is made of, make one. Go ahead—it's easy!

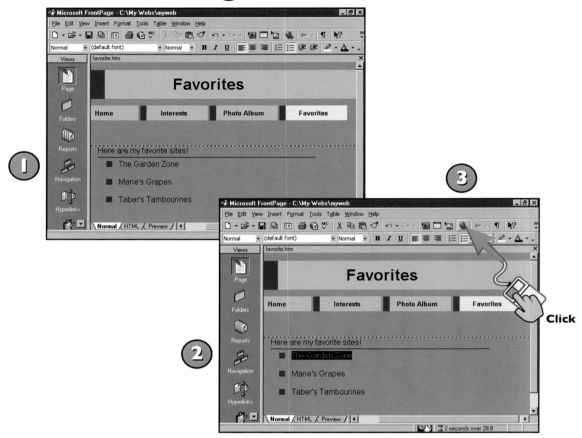

✓ Try to keep the link source short. If the link will be text that's within a paragraph a few lines long, don't highlight the whole paragraph in step 1; just select an appropriate word or two to serve as the link source.

✓ See Task 9 to learn about using a picture as a link source.

Click

1 Type and format the text that will serve as the link source.

2 Select the text.

3 Click the **Hyperlink** button on the Standard toolbar.

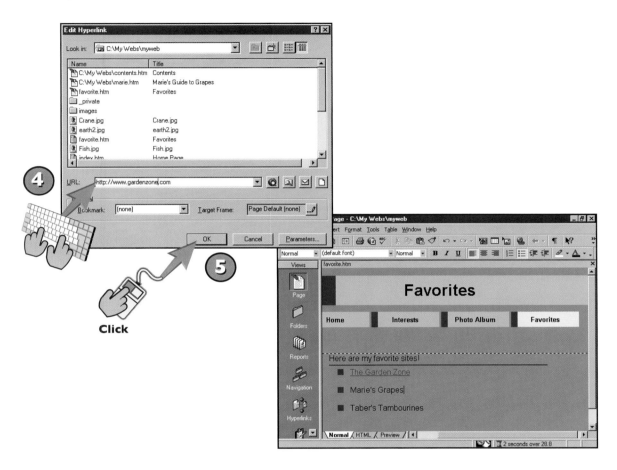

Click

(4) In the box labeled **URL**, type the URL of the page to which the link leads (note that FrontPage has already typed the http:// part for you).

(5) Click **OK**.

✅ After finishing a text link, avoid monkeying with the character formatting of the link source text. Browsers display link source text with unique formatting (usually blue and underlined) to help the visitor instantly identify links. You don't want your character formatting to make your links hard for visitors to see.

Task 3: Creating a Link to a URL You Can't Remember

Know where you want to link to, but can't remember the exact URL? That's a problem, because if there's even one mistake in the URL, the link won't work properly. To help you get it right, FrontPage lets you use your browser to surf to a page and then instantly copy the URL into the Create Hyperlink box.

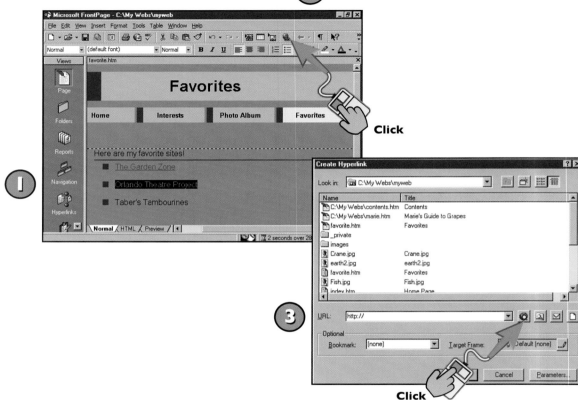

✓ After you finish this task, you can close your Web browser or leave it open—it doesn't matter.

1 Type and format the text that will serve as the link source and select it.

2 Click the **Hyperlink** button on the Standard toolbar.

3 Click the button immediately to the right of the URL box ("Use your Web browser to select a page or file"). Your Web browser opens.

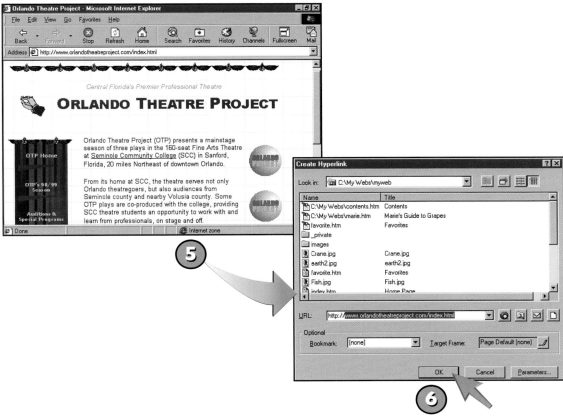

(4) Surf to the page to which you want to link.

(5) While viewing the right page, press and hold your **Alt** key, press your **Tab** key, and release both keys.

(6) Click **OK** in the Create Hyperlink dialog box.

✅ **Depending on the way your PC and Internet software are set up, you may need to connect to the Internet between step 3 and step 4.**

Task 4: Linking to Files So Your Visitors Can Download Them

You may have content that you want to offer your visitors, but don't want to turn into a Web page. For example, if you have a long story, report, or other document in a word processing file, it may be better to offer that file for downloading instead of turning it into a Web page. You can offer any kind of computer file for downloading—documents, pictures, and so on.

To use a file you provide, the visitor must have the right program. For example, if you publish a Word file, the visitor must have a program that can display Word files to view it. There's not much you can do about this, except to try to offer only popular, widely supported file types.

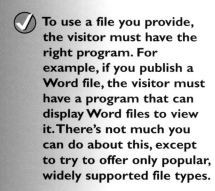

Click

Click

1. Prepare the file to which you want to link and create the link source in your Web page.

2. Select the link source, and then click the **Hyperlink** button on the Standard toolbar.

3. Click the **Make a hyperlink to a file on your computer** button (second button to the right of the URL box).

Next Step

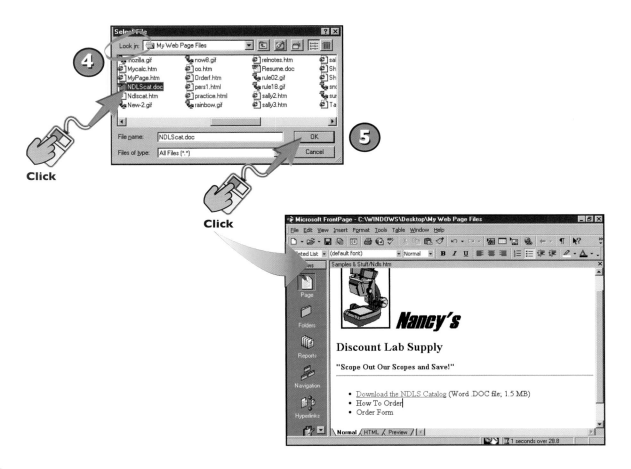

Click

Click

In the link source text (or near it), it's courteous to tell your visitors the file type (so they can tell whether it's a file they're equipped to view) and size (so they can guesstimate how long it will take to download at the speed of their Internet connection).

④ Use the **Look in** list and folders to open the folder in which the file is stored and click the file's name.

⑤ Click **OK** in the Select File dialog box.

When you publish your page to the Web, make sure the file you're linking to gets copied to the Web, too (see Part 12, "Publishing Your Page Online").

Task 5: Linking to an Email Address

A *signature* tells visitors who created (or manages) the page. Often, the signature includes a *mailto* link, one that points to the email address of the Web page author. If the visitor's browser is integrated with email, clicking that link opens the email program and a new message, automatically pre-addressed to the email address in the link. Create mailto links for signatures, or anywhere you want to help your visitor conveniently send email.

A mailto link isn't the only way your visitors can contact you. You can also provide a response form that enables visitors to send you questions or comments right from the Web page, without opening their email programs. See Part 11, "Adding Fill-in-the-Blank Forms."

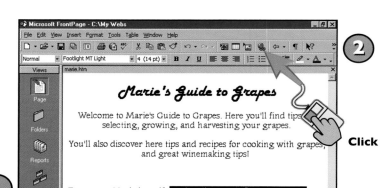

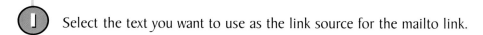

Select the text you want to use as the link source for the mailto link.

Click the **Hyperlink** button on the Standard toolbar.

Click the **Make a hyperlink that sends Email** button (third button to the right of the URL box).

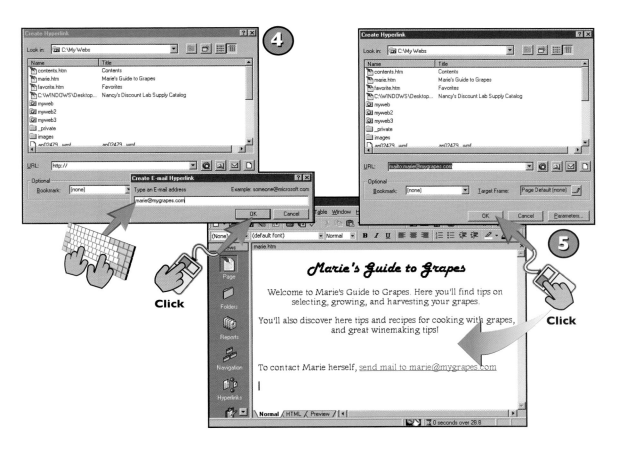

Click

Click

④ Type the email address, and click **OK**.

⑤ Click **OK** in the Create Hyperlink dialog box.

✔ Some visitors use browsers that don't support mailto links; they see the link source, but nothing happens when they click it. So even if you supply a mailto link like this one, make sure always to show the full address in the link source or elsewhere nearby, so those folks can read it and type it into their email programs.

End Task

Task 6: Creating Bookmarks to Link To

Links don't always lead to other pages or files. In a long or complex page, a link may lead to another part of the same page. Those links work because of *bookmarks* inserted in specific spots within the page.

Bookmarks are a great way to help your visitors easily navigate a long page, such as detailed index, glossary, or frequently asked questions (FAQ) file. After you create all of the bookmarks you need, see Task 7, to learn how to link to them.

If there's unique text at each point where you'll put a bookmark (for example, unique section headings in a long page), save time by selecting that text and then performing step 2. The selected text appears automatically as the bookmark name. When you create a bookmark this way, no flag appears in page view; instead, the text gets a dashed underline (invisible online).

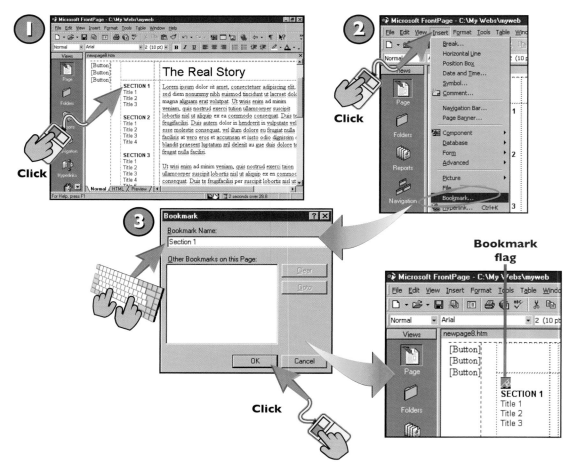

Bookmark flag

Click a spot where you'd like a link to lead.

Click **Insert**, and then choose **Bookmark**.

Type a name for this bookmark, and click **OK**.

Task 7: Linking to a Bookmark

Start Here

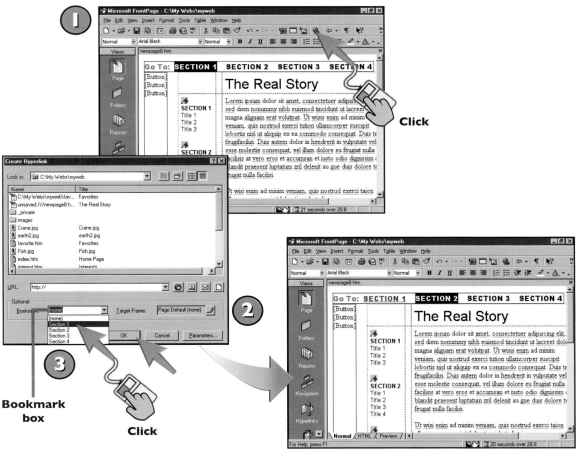

Click

Bookmark box

Click

Once you've inserted your bookmarks, you create links to them as easily as you can to anything else—easier, actually. Note that you can link from anywhere on a page to bookmarks elsewhere in the same page (as you do in this task), or from one page to bookmarks in another (see Part 9, "Building a Web").

Note that what FrontPage calls a "bookmark" is often called an "anchor" or a "target" in other Web authoring programs. And just to make things really confusing, the Netscape Navigator browser calls the shortcuts users create to easily go to Web pages "bookmarks."

1. Create and select the link source, as you would when creating any kind of link, and then click the **Hyperlink** button.

2. Click the arrow on the right end of the Bookmark box.

3. In the list, click the name of the bookmark you want this link to lead to, and then click **OK**.

End Task

Task 8: Editing Links

No matter what kind of link it is, you can change it later. You can even change one kind of link into another; for example, you can change a link to a URL into a mailto link.

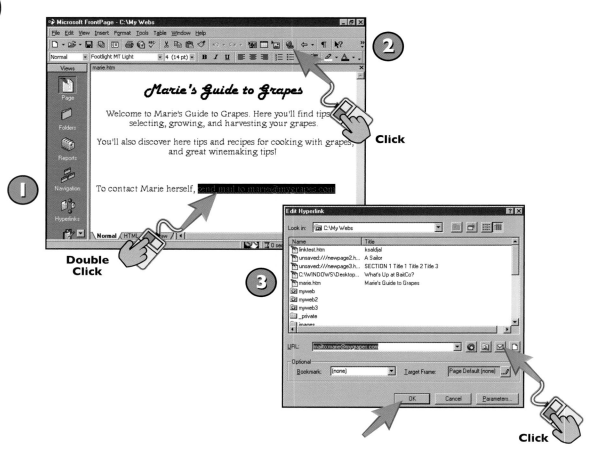

Click

Double
Click

✓ In both the Edit Hyperlink and Create Hyperlink dialog boxes, note that there's an arrow on the right side of the URL box. To conveniently link to a URL you've recently used for another link, click the arrow, and then choose the URL from the list that appears.

Click

① While viewing the page in the Normal tab, double-click the link to select it.

② Click the **Hyperlink** button.

③ Change anything you want on the Edit Hyperlink dialog box (which is identical to the Create Hyperlink dialog box, except for its name), and then click **OK**.

Task 9: Using a Picture as a Link

Start Here

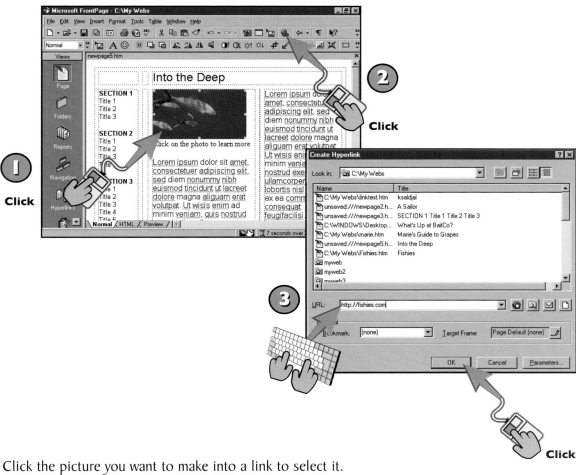

Click

Click

Click

Click

Creating a picture link is exactly like creating a text link—the sole difference is that you start out by selecting a picture, not text. (Don't worry about not knowing how to add pictures yet—Part 6, "Adding and Formatting Pictures," is coming. In the meantime, you can practice with any pictures your template may have given you, or just skip this task and return after Part 6.)

(1) Click the picture you want to make into a link to select it.

(2) Click the **Hyperlink** button on the Standard toolbar.

(3) Create a link to a URL, a file, an email address, or a bookmark exactly as shown in previous tasks.

✓ This is just the tip of the iceberg for picture links. In Part 6, you'll learn how to put multiple links all in one picture, so that clicking different parts of the picture activates different links. This feature is called *hotspots*.

End Task

Task 10: Testing Your Links

Sure, to test your URLs you can preview the page in either the Preview tab or your browser (see Part 2, "Starting (and Saving) New Web Pages"), and then click 'em. But while you're in the thick of editing your page, there's a faster way.

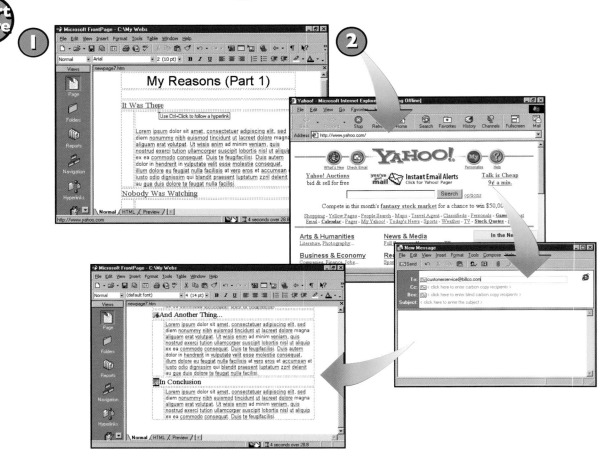

✓ Depending on the way your PC and Internet software are set up, you may need to connect to the Internet after step 2 if the link points to a Web page.

1 Viewing your page in **Normal** tab, press and hold the **Ctrl** key.

2 Point to the link, click, and then release the **Ctrl** key.

If the link leads to a Web page, your Web browser opens and goes to the URL.

If the link leads to an email address, your email program opens and starts a new message.

If the link leads to a file, Windows opens whatever program it needs to display that file.

If the link leads to a bookmark, no program opens, and FrontPage scrolls to where that bookmark appears.

End Task

Task 11: Removing Links

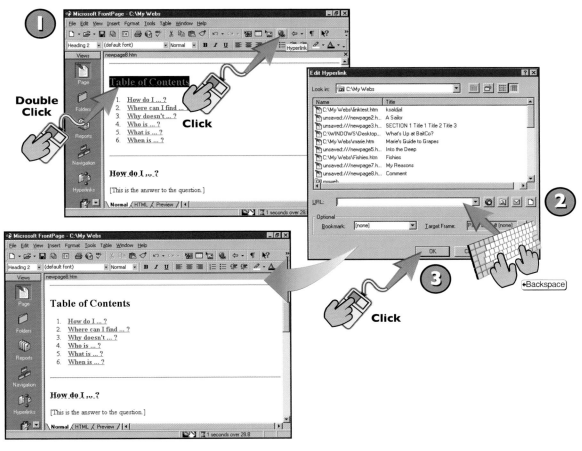

Suppose you attach a link to text or a picture, and then decide you want to keep that text or picture but don't want it to be a link anymore. FrontPage does not make it immediately obvious how one "de-links" text or a picture. So here's how.

✓ These steps work for any type of link—URL, email, file, and so on.

✓ If you want to get rid of the link *and* the link source (the text or picture that activates the link), just delete the link source. The link goes away with it.

(1) While viewing the page in the Normal tab, double-click the link to select it, and then click the **Hyperlink** button.

(2) Press your **Backspace** key until the URL box is *completely* empty. (You must delete even the http:// part or any other prefix in the URL box.)

(3) Click **OK**.

Task 12: Linking to Your Own Web Pages

Again, the best way to link among your own pages is to build them together as a web, as you'll do in Part 9. Doing so lets you easily manage the links, build navigation bars, and do other stuff that enhances the usability of your site. But no law says you have to build a web just to link two pages together.

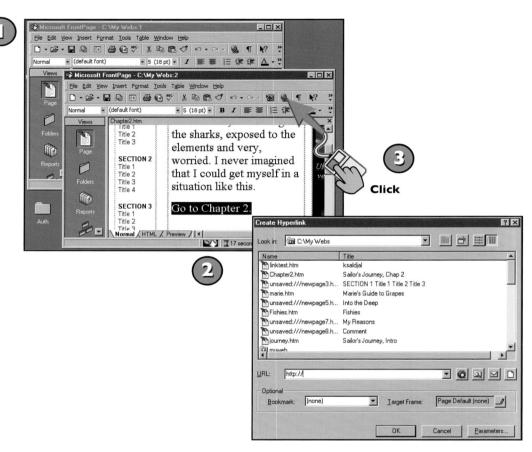

✓ When you publish, you must make sure that you publish the page and all pages to which it links (see Part 12).

1. Create both Web pages.

2. Open the page in which you will create the link, and select the link source.

3. Click the **Hyperlink** button on the Standard toolbar.

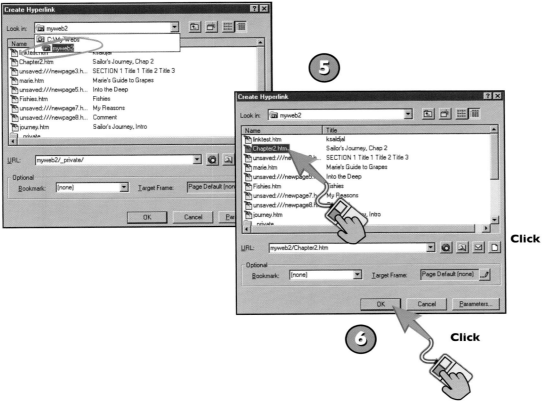

Click

Click

④ Use the **Look in** list and the folders beneath it to navigate to the folder in which the page you're linking to is stored.

⑤ In the list of files, click the name of the page to which you're linking.

⑥ Click **OK**.

✓ After creating the link (but with the page containing the link still open in Page view), click the **Hyperlinks** button in the Views bar to see a map of the links in the page and where they lead. You'll learn more about using the Hyperlinks view in **Part 9**.

Adding and Formatting Pictures

The pictures and other graphical elements in your pages add not only useful content but also style. Even better, adding pictures is easier than you might think. In this part, you'll learn not only how to add pictures, but also how to make them look great. (Part 7, "Using Borders, Backgrounds, Sounds, and Other Fun Stuff," builds upon this part, showing you still more ways to dress up your page with graphics, sound, and motion.)

While adding pictures to your pages, keep in mind that every picture lengthens the time it takes the page to fully materialize on a visitor's screen.

You know from your own surfing trips how frustrating a slow Web page is, especially when it's slow just because it has too many pictures. (In Part 12, "Publishing Your Page Online," you'll learn how FrontPage 2000 helps you predict the online performance of your page, so you can fine-tune it before you publish.) In this part and in Part 7, I'll help you make the choices that will make your pages both beautiful *and* quick.

Tasks

Task 1: Inserting Clip Art

Sometimes, you don't have anything specific you need to put in a picture, but you want some pictures to appear in your page to dress it up. That's when FrontPage 2000's built-in Clip Gallery comes in handy. The Clip Gallery lets you quickly add to a page any item from the FrontPage (or Office 2000) clip library, which contains thousands of graphics, photos, sound clips, and animations.

To expand your clip library with new pictures, click Clip Gallery's **Clips Online** button. That button opens your default Web browser and Internet connection and goes to a Microsoft Web site with additional clips.

After clicking a category, if you don't like what you see, click the **Back** button on Clip Gallery's toolbar to return to the category icons to try another.

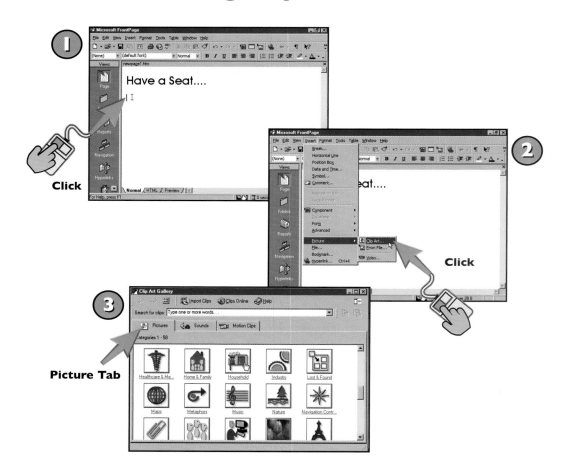

Click in your page at the general spot where you want to insert the clip art.

Click **Insert**, choose **Picture**, and then choose **Clip Art**.

Scroll through the categories listed in the Picture tab and click on a likely-looking category to display miniature versions (*thumbnails*) of the pictures in that group.

Next Step

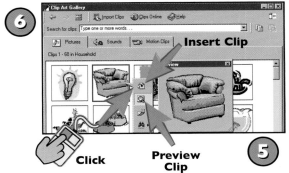

Insert Clip

Have a Seat....

✔ When you save the page, a dialog box appears to report that all picture files will be copied to the same folder as the Web page file (see Task 3). Click **OK**.

✔ After you insert a clip, you can change that clip's appearance or position in any of the ways described later in this part, including changing the clip's size, repositioning it, or giving it a border.

④ Scroll through the pictures shown. When you see a picture you like, click it once.

⑤ To get a better (bigger) look at the clip before choosing to insert it, click **Preview Clip**.

⑥ Click **Insert Clip** to insert the clip art in your Web page.

Task 2: Searching for Clip Art

Given the thousands of clips available in the clip art library, finding the one you want by browsing the categories can be a pain. Fortunately, every clip in the library has descriptive keywords attached to it. The Gallery includes a search tool that can narrow the clips shown to only the ones whose keywords match a word you type. That makes finding a clip relating to a particular subject a snap.

✓ You can type more than one word in the Search for clips box (for example, "circus clown") to narrow the search even further. But one well-chosen word usually works best.

✓ You can also search for clips by browsing to a clip (see Task 1) that's in the right ballpark, clicking it, and then clicking the **Find Similar Clips** button to narrow the display to only clips who have keywords in common with the clip you clicked.

Start Here

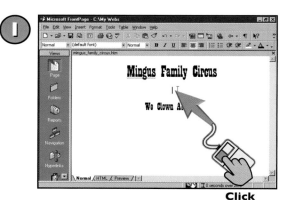
Click

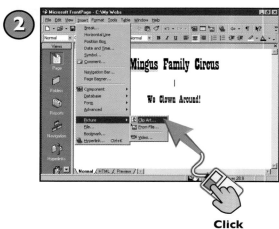
Click

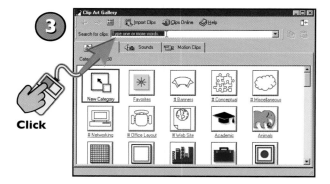
Click

(1) Click in your page at the spot where you want to insert the clip art.

(2) Click **Insert,** choose **Picture**, and then choose **Clip Art.**

(3) Click in the **Search for clips** box.

Next Step

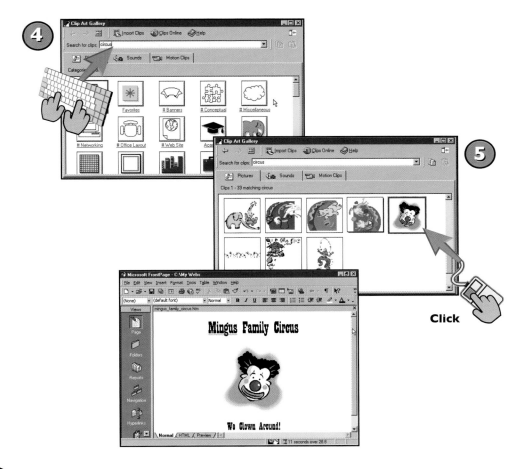

Click

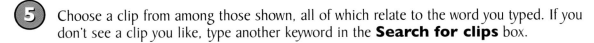

(4) Type a word describing the general subject you want the clips to relate to, and then press
Enter.

(5) Choose a clip from among those shown, all of which relate to the word you typed. If you
don't see a clip you like, type another keyword in the **Search for clips** box.

✓ After step 4, all tabs in the
Clip Gallery—Pictures,
Sounds, and Motion Clips—
show only the files whose
keywords match the word
you typed.

✓ If you scroll to the bottom
of the Clip Gallery after
step 4, you may see a link
labeled **Keep Looking**.
Clicking this link displays
another set of clips related
to the word you typed, but
not as closely as the first
set of files shown.

End
Task

Task 3: Inserting a Picture from a File

Start Here

Got a picture file of your own ready to drop in your page? If so, here you go. (If not, Tasks 4, 5 and 6 will help you get one.) Ideally, any picture file you use in a Web page will be in **GIF** or **JPEG** file format (using the file extension .gif or .jpg). But you may use pictures stored in just about any file format, including .png, .bmp, .tif, .pcx, .wmf, and others.

Insert Picture From File

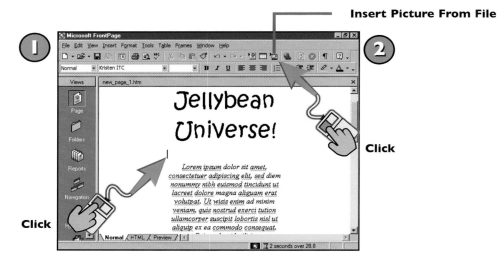

Click

Click

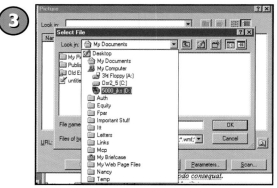

✓ **Don't worry too much about exactly where you position the picture. After inserting it, you can fine-tune its location, size, shape, and more, as you learn to do later in this part.**

1️⃣ Open the Web page in Page view and click at the spot where you want the picture.

2️⃣ Click the **Insert Picture from File** button on the **Standard** toolbar.

3️⃣ Use the **Look in** list to navigate to the folder where the picture is stored.

Next Step

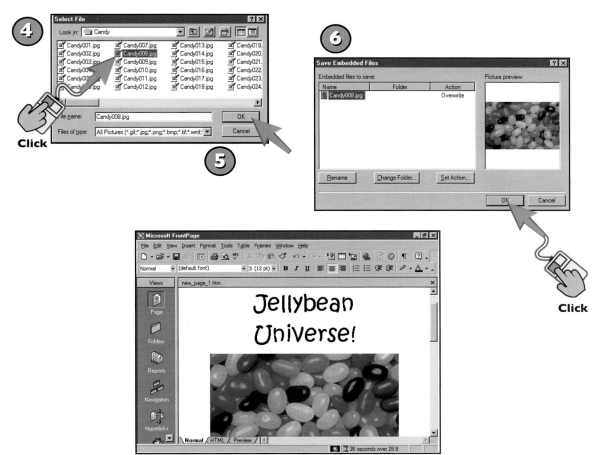

Click (on Select File dialog)

Click (on OK button, step 5)

If the picture you're inserting is not already in **GIF, JPEG, or PNG** format, its name won't appear at first in the list that appears after step 3. To make it appear, open the **Files of type** list in the **Select File** dialog box, and then choose the file's type (or choose **All Files**).

Picture files you've inserted that are not already in **GIF** or **JPEG** format are automatically converted to **GIF** when FrontPage copies them to the Web page's folder.

4 Click the picture's name.

5 Click **OK**.

6 When you save the page, a dialog box appears to report that the picture files will be copied to the same folder as the Web page file. Click **OK.**

Task 4: Creating a Picture

You can create your own Web page pictures with almost any draw or paint program. Ideally, you should check your program's File menu for an Export or Save As item you can use to save your creations in GIF or JPEG format—but if there's no such option, FrontPage can convert most other formats to GIF (see Task 3). The next steps demonstrate how easy it is to create a picture with Paint, a program included in every copy of Windows 95/98/NT.

The Premium edition of Office 2000 includes Microsoft PhotoDraw, a great program for creating new pictures and saving them in GIF or JPEG format. The standalone version of FrontPage 2000 includes Image Composer.

Start Here

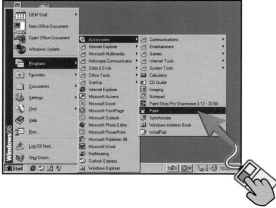

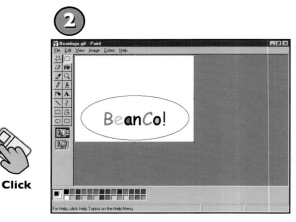

Click

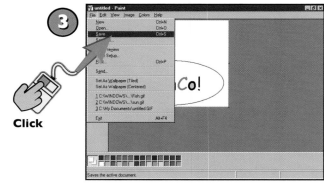

Click

1 Click **Start**, and then choose **Programs**, **Accessories**, **Paint**.

2 Use Paint's tools to create your masterpiece.

3 When it's time to save your creation, click **File**, and then choose **Save**.

Next Step

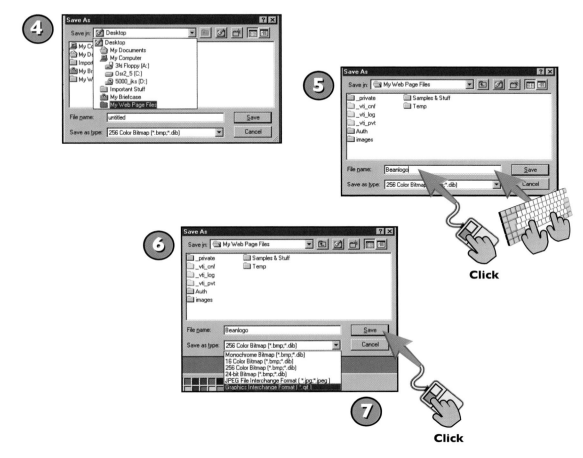

Click

Click

If your program lets you choose the resolution and number of colors (*color depth*) of a picture, note that although high resolutions and color depths make pictures look better, they also make the picture file larger, slowing down the display of your page. Resolutions between 75 and 100 *dpi* (dots per inch) and a color depth of 16 or 256 colors is fine for most Web graphics.

If the program you use can't save in GIF or JPEG format, and you find that FrontPage can't import the file format your program produces, look in your program for a Save As or Export item, and try saving the file in another popular format FrontPage *can* convert, such as .bmp, .pcx or .tif.

4 Use the **Save in** list to select the folder where you store the Web page in which you will use this picture.

5 Type a short filename for your creation. (Don't type any *filename extension*—a period and three letters at the end.)

6 Drop down the **Save as Type** list, and choose **Graphics Interchange Format (*.gif)**.

7 Click **Save**.

Task 5: Scanning a Picture into a Page

Got a scanner hooked up to your PC? Then you can scan pictures directly into your Web pages in FrontPage 2000. Here's how.

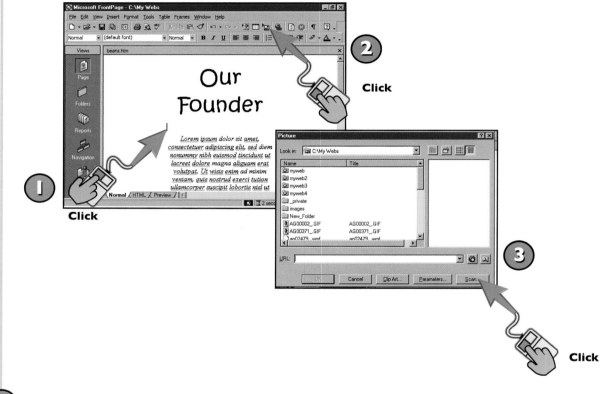

Click

Click

Click

Click

✓ If you have a digital camera whose software installs in Windows as a **TWAIN**-compliant device (most do), use the steps in this task to insert your digital photos. If your camera's software is not **TWAIN**-compliant, use it to save pictures on your hard disk in **GIF** or another popular format, and then insert the picture file as shown in Task 3.

1 Open the Web page in FrontPage's Page view, and click the spot where you want the picture.

2 Click the **Insert Picture from File** button on the **Standard** toolbar, and then click **Cancel** to close the Select File dialog box.

3 Click the **Scan** button.

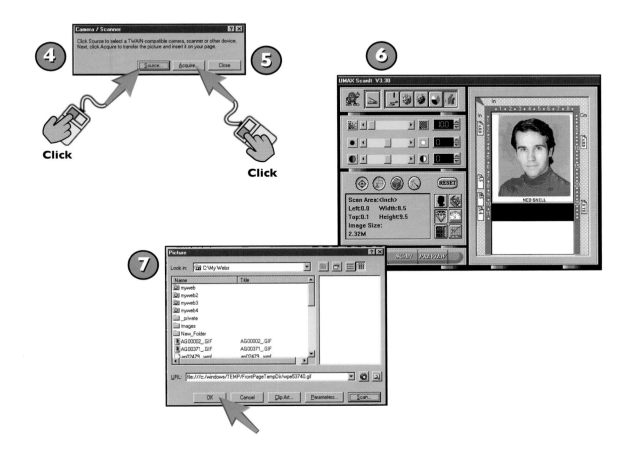

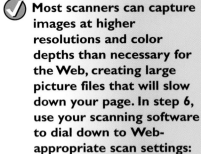

(4) Click **Source** to open a list of scanners and digital cameras configured on your PC, and click the one you want to use.

(5) Click **Acquire** to open your scanner's control program. (It may look different from the one shown.)

(6) Choose from your scanning options, and then scan.

(7) After scanning, click **OK** to close the Picture dialog box and insert the scanned picture.

✔️ **Most scanners can capture images at higher resolutions and color depths than necessary for the Web, creating large picture files that will slow down your page. In step 6, use your scanning software to dial down to Web-appropriate scan settings: 75–100 dpi resolution, 16–256 colors.**

End Task

Task 6: Getting Pictures from Web Clip Libraries

If you want a picture that's not in the clip art library, and you don't want to create or scan it, another resource is the Internet, where you can find online libraries bursting with clip art goodies for downloading. Here's an example of how to access and use online clip art. (After picking up pictures this way, you insert the files in a page as described in Task 3.)

Some clip art you must pay for, some is free, and some is free with strings attached—for example, some sites let you use their clip art free as long as you include text next to it crediting the artist. Always read and follow all copyright notices and other usage instructions on any page from which you download clip art.

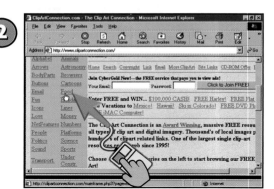

Click

Right
Click

1 In your Web browser, go to a good clip art library or site; one choice is www.clipartconnection.com.

2 Click through the categories to locate an image you want to use.

3 While viewing the clip art in your browser, right-click the picture you want to use.

Next Step

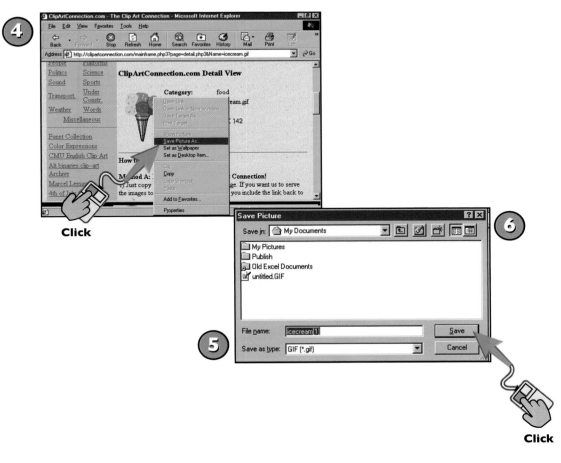

Click

Click

✓ A good way to find tons of clip art sites is to do a search with Yahoo (www.yahoo.com), Excite (www.excite.com) or another search page, using **web clip art** as a search term.

✓ Remember: It doesn't really matter where you save the picture in step 5, as long as you can remember its location. When you insert the picture (see Task 3), the picture file is copied automatically to the page's folder.

✓ If the picture you want to use is in a clip art library you obtained on disk or CD-ROM, copy the picture file from there to the folder where your Web page files are stored, and then insert the picture as shown in Task 3.

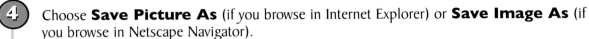

4 Choose **Save Picture As** (if you browse in Internet Explorer) or **Save Image As** (if you browse in Netscape Navigator).

5 Choose any convenient folder in which to store the picture.

6 Click **Save**.

End Task

Task 7: Replacing a Picture

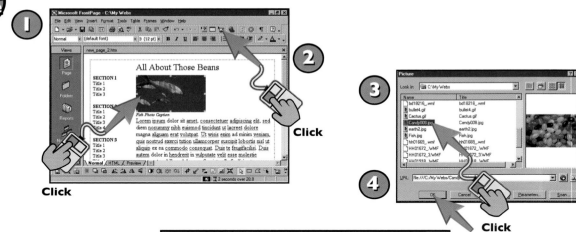

Oooops... **Turns out you didn't want that picture after all. Here's how to replace it. (These steps also come in handy for replacing pictures left in the page by a template with new pictures you've hand-picked.)**

Click

Click

Click

Click

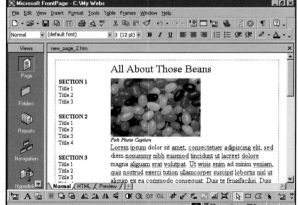

✓ **To deselect a picture after working with it, just click anywhere in the page except on the picture.**

✓ **To delete a picture without replacing it, just click it to select it, and then press the Delete key on your keyboard.**

1. Click the picture to select it. *Handles*—little squares—appear around the picture to show it's selected.

2. Click the **Insert Picture from File** button.

3. Choose a new picture file, or click **Clip Art** to choose from the **Clip Gallery**, or click **Scan** to scan the replacement picture.

4. Click **OK** in the Picture dialog box.

Task 8: Changing the Size of a Picture

Start Here

Click

Click

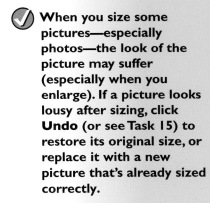

Suppose that after you insert a picture, you feel it's too large or too small? No problem—you can change its size right from within Page view.

✓ When you size some pictures—especially photos—the look of the picture may suffer (especially when you enlarge). If a picture looks lousy after sizing, click **Undo** (or see Task 15) to restore its original size, or replace it with a new picture that's already sized correctly.

✓ You may be able to improve the appearance of a picture after changing its size by selecting the picture and then clicking the **Resample** button on the **Picture** toolbar.

1 Click the picture to select it. *Handles*—little squares—appear around the picture to show it's selected.

2 Click and hold on a corner handle—*not* a side, top, or bottom handle.

3 **Drag** toward the picture's center (to shrink it) or away from the center (to enlarge it), and then release the mouse button.

End Task

Task 9: Changing the Shape of a Picture

You can also stretch a picture out of its original shape. You might do this to change the look of an abstract graphic or to create a fun, funky effect with a photo. Give it a try.

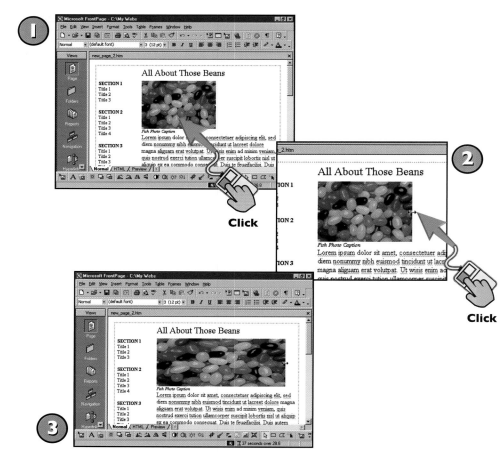

Start Here

Click

Click

Don't like the way the picture looks after you reshape it? Don't fiddle with trying to drag it back into shape. Just click **Undo**. If that doesn't work, see Task 15.

1 Click the picture to select it and display its handles.

2 Click and hold a side handle (to change width) or top or bottom handle (to change height).

3 Drag toward the picture's center (to reduce width or height) or away from center (to increase width or height), and then release the mouse button.

End Task

Task 10: Cropping a Picture

Start Here

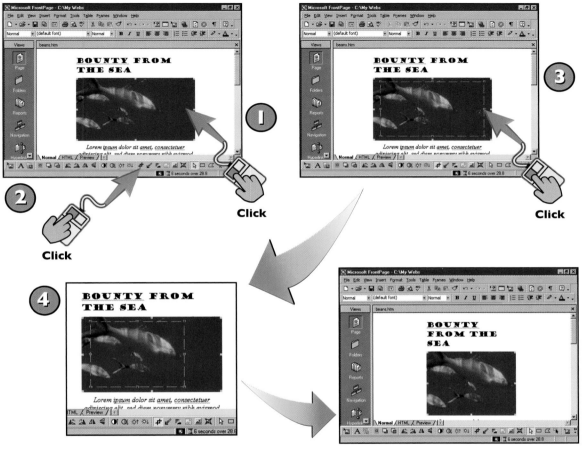

Click

Click

Click

Whenever you can, you should *crop* a picture—trim unwanted regions off the sides, top, and bottom—in the program in which it was created before inserting it in a page. But when that's not possible, FrontPage lets you trim up a picture right in Page view.

① Click the picture to select it.

② Click the **Crop** button on the **Picture** toolbar. A dashed line appears around the image, showing its own set of cropping handles.

③ Drag the cropping handles so that the outline surrounds only the part of the image you wish to keep.

④ Click the **Crop** button again to complete the crop.

To crop both one side and the top or bottom in one move, click and hold on a corner handle in step 3.

End Task

Task 11: Rotating or Flipping a Picture

Start Here

Okay, so you've got a picture that's just what you want, except it's sideways, upside down, or backward (or it's fine, but you *want* it to be sideways, upside down, or backward). No problem. *Rotating* can turn a sideways or upside down picture the right way, and *flipping* a picture reverses it, as if it were a slide or transparency and you flipped it over in the projector.

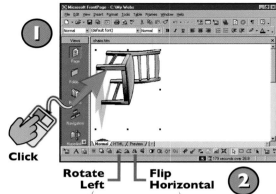

Click

Rotate Left | Flip Horizontal

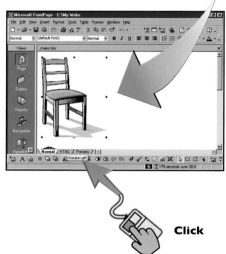 

Click | Click

✓ Think of it this way: If the picture is upside down (but *not* backward), click a Rotate button (either one will do) twice. If the picture is upside down *and* backward, click **Flip Vertical** once. If the picture is backward but *not* upside down, click **Flip Horizontal** once.

✓ Click **Undo** to quickly fix rotation or flipping goofs.

1 Click the picture to select it.

2 Click a button on the **Picture** toolbar:

> Click **Rotate Left** or **Rotate Right** to rotate 90 degrees. (Click again to go another 90 degrees.)

> Click **Flip Horizontal** or **Flip Vertical** to reverse the image.

End Task

Task 12: Changing the Contrast or Brightness of a Picture

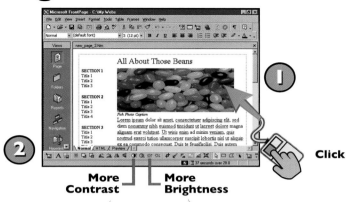

With some types of picture files, you can adjust the *contrast* (the degree of distinction between light and dark) and brightness of the picture from within FrontPage. Note that this won't work with very simple graphical images, but often works with photos or other images that contain many different shades.

More Contrast   **More Brightness**

Click   **Click**

① Click the picture to select it.

② Click a button on the **Picture** toolbar:

    To adjust the contrast, click **More Contrast** or **Less Contrast**.

    To adjust the brightness level, click **More Brightness** or **Less Brightness**.

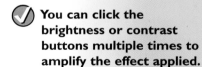 You can click the brightness or contrast buttons multiple times to amplify the effect applied.

 If you click any of these buttons several times in a row and see no apparent change in the picture, the picture is of a type whose brightness and contrast cannot be adjusted.

Task 13: Changing to Black and White or "Washing Out" Color

On the Web, where so many authors assault you with color overkill, carefully selected black and white images—which typically also contain shades of gray, like a black and white TV image—add a touch of class. Another cool effect is "washing out"—fading the colors in a picture so they're softer, more muted. In FrontPage, you can easily apply either of these elegant effects to any picture.

✓ After going to black and white or washing out, you may want to adjust the picture's contrast and/or brightness (see Task 12).

✓ Going black and white or washing out often has a side benefit: It may reduce the size of the picture file, so your page shows up more quickly on a visitor's screen.

Start Here

①

Click

② Black & White | Wash Out

Click

Click

① Click the picture to select it.

② Click a button on the **Picture** toolbar:

> To change the picture to black and white, click the **Black and White** button.
>
> To wash out the colors, click the **Wash Out** button.

End Task

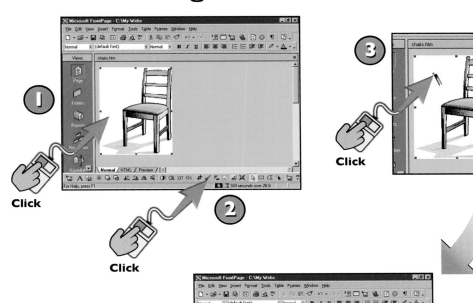

Click

Click

Click

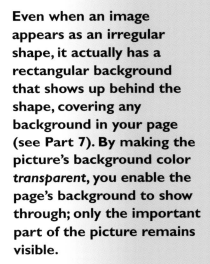

Even when an image appears as an irregular shape, it actually has a rectangular background that shows up behind the shape, covering any background in your page (see Part 7). By making the picture's background color *transparent*, you enable the page's background to show through; only the important part of the picture remains visible.

✓ In step 3, the pointer looks like a pencil eraser because you will "erase" the color you click.

✓ If you set a transparent color for a picture that is not currently in **GIF** format, FrontPage reports that it must convert the picture to GIF in order to set transparency after step 3. Click **OK** to complete the conversion.

(1) Click the picture to select it.

(2) Click the **Set Transparent Color** button on the **Picture** toolbar.

(3) Carefully point to the picture's background, and click.

Task 15: Undoing Everything You've Done to a Picture

Sometimes you'll monkey around with a picture so much that you wind up wishing you could erase all of your changes and restore the original, unaltered picture. In such cases, Undo often won't do—too many changes under the bridge. But in just two steps, you can remove all sizing, shaping, cropping, transparency, brightness/contrast changes, rotation, flipping, black-and-whiting, and washing out.

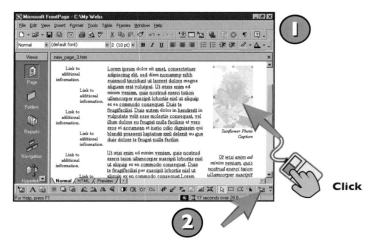

Click

✓ If you want to remove some, but not all, of the changes you've made to a picture, use the Undo list or selectively change the formatting however you wish.

1 Click the picture to select it.

2 Click the **Restore** button on the **Picture** toolbar.

Task 16: Choosing a Picture's Alignment

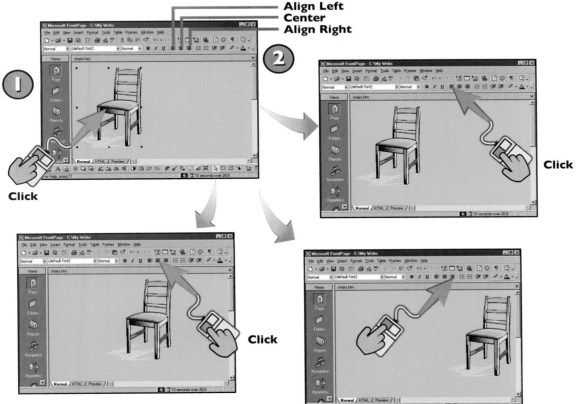

Align Left
Center
Align Right

Click

Click

Click

Click

By default, a picture you insert goes on the left side of the page. But you can center it or align it to the right side of the page, exactly as you do text.

① Click the picture to select it.

② Click one of the alignment buttons on the Formatting toolbar: **Align Left**, **Center**, or **Align Right**.

✓ For all intents and purposes, a picture is a paragraph. That means you can not only use the Alignment buttons to align it as you would a text paragraph, but also that you can indent pictures with the Increase Indent button.

Task 17: Changing the Position of a Picture

Generally, you position a picture only in the ways you position a paragraph; it can go at the top of the page, at the bottom, or between any two paragraphs, and it can be aligned to the left, right, or center. There are exceptions, which you'll explore in Tasks 18—20. But here are the simple steps for moving a picture from one general location to another.

✓ To drag to a spot below the visible part of the page, drag slowly toward the bottom. When you see the page begin to scroll, stop dragging, but don't release the button. When the spot where the picture belongs scrolls into view, drag upward slightly to stop the scrolling, point to the spot, and release.

✓ Alternatively, you can move a picture with cut and paste, just like text. Select the picture, click the Cut button, click in the new spot, and click Paste.

Start Here

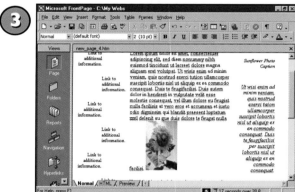

Click

1 Click and hold on the picture.

2 Drag to where you want it. (A little square icon follows the pointer to tell you you're dragging something.)

3 Release the mouse button.

End Task

Task 18: Wrapping Text to a Picture

Start Here

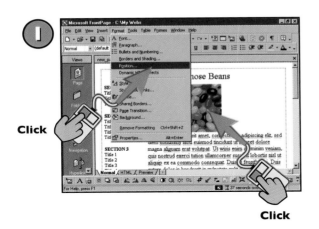

Click

Click

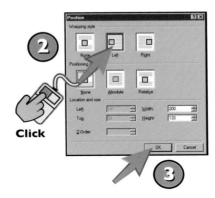

Click

When text comes right after a picture, you can choose the relationship between the text and picture—should the text start below the image, to the right of it, or to the left of it?

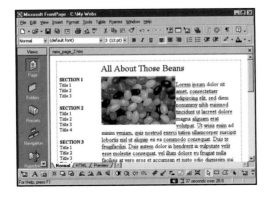

(1) Click the picture to select it, click **Format**, and then choose **Position**.

(2) Click the wrapping style you want from the three Wrapping Styles at the top of the dialog box.

(3) Click **OK**.

✅ You can't use a wrapping style with a picture that's *absolutely positioned* (see Task 19). If you apply this task to an absolutely positioned picture, the absolute positioning is removed automatically, and the picture reverts to standard positioning.

End Task

Page
117

Task 19: Choosing the "Absolute" Position of a Picture

Using this task, you can position a picture at a precise spot on the page, just as you might in a desktop publishing program. This "absolute positioning" gives you far greater control of your page layout.

This positioning shows up *only* when the page is viewed through a DHTML-compatible browser, such as Internet Explorer 4 (or later) or Navigator 4 (or later). Use this task only for pages that will be published on an intranet or other controlled environment.

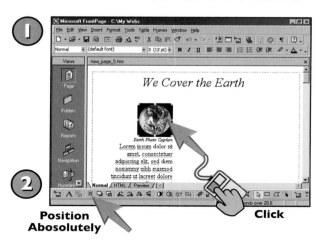

Start Here

Position Absolutely

Click

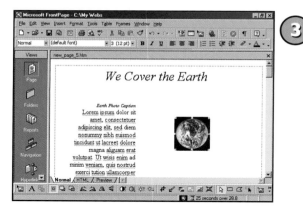

✓ **Tip**
Note that you can drag an absolutely positioned picture on top of text, other pictures, or anything else on the page. To learn how to control the way these objects overlap, see Task 20.

① Click the picture to select it.

② Click the **Position Absolutely** button on the **Picture** toolbar.

③ Drag the picture to any spot you like.

End Task

Task 20: Layering Pictures on Top of One Another

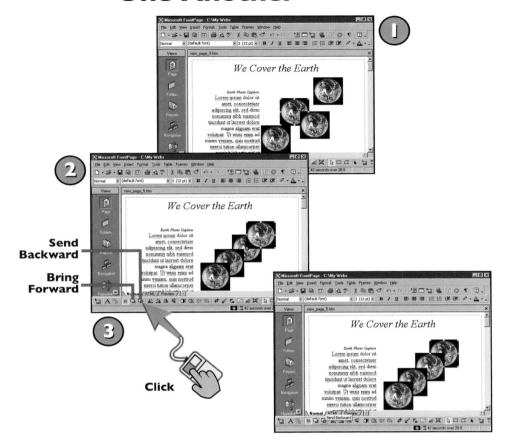

Send Backward

Bring Forward

Click

You can lay an absolutely positioned picture (see Task 12) on top of other pictures or text in the page. But suppose you want the object underneath the absolutely positioned picture to appear on top of the picture? Here's how to control the order of *layers* you can create with absolutely positioned objects.

(1) Drag your absolutely positioned object or objects on top of one another, in any order.

(2) Click any visible portion of the object whose position in the pile you want to change.

(3) On the **Picture** toolbar, click **Bring Forward** to move the object one level closer to the top of the pile, or click **Send Backward** to move the object one level deeper.

 If the object you want to work on is completely hidden (so you can't select it), use **Send Backward** on other objects to move them beneath the one you want.

Task 21: Putting Multiple Links in a Picture

A picture containing multiple links is called an *imagemap* in general Web authoring parlance. To make one in FrontPage, the word to remember is *hotspots*—invisible boxes on the picture, each of which has a link attached to it.

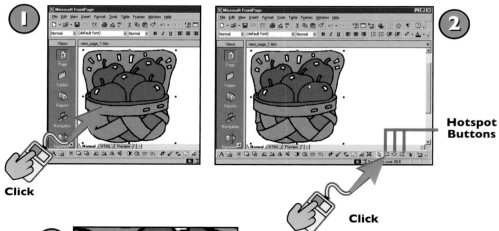

Click

Hotspot Buttons

Click

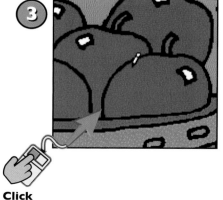

Click

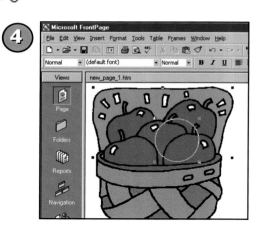

Click

✓ Choose a picture that has easily identifiable regions in it to help visitors guess where the links are.

✓ As much as possible, complete the positioning, sizing, and other formatting of the picture before adding hotspots.

✓ In steps 3 and 4, don't worry about making the hotspot perfectly fit the region or lay perfectly in top of the region; you'll fine-tune its size and position later.

① Click the picture to select it.

② Click the **Hotspot** button that most closely matches the shape of the first region: **Rectangular Hotspot**, **Circular Hotspot**, or **Polygonal Regional**

③ Point to a spot on the picture in or near the region.

④ Click and hold, drag outward to create a shape roughly the size of the region, and then release the mouse button.

Next Step

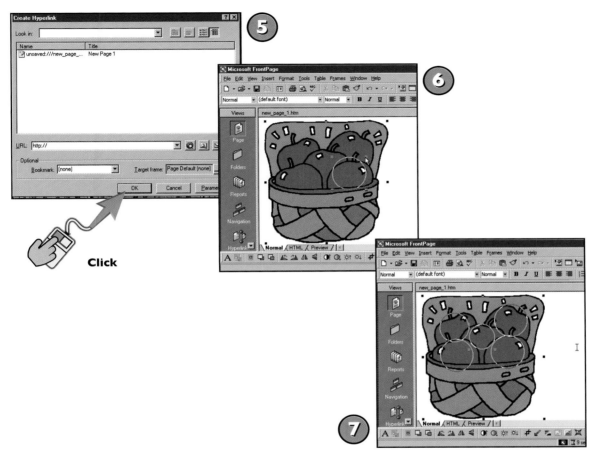

Click

⑤ Complete the **Create Hyperlink** dialog box exactly as you would to create any other link (see Part 5, "Making Hyperlinks"), and then click **OK**.

⑥ Adjust the hotspot using its handles so its size and position fit the region (more or less).

⑦ Repeat steps 2–6 for each link in the picture, creating a separate hotspot for each.

✅ To use the Polygonal hotspot tool to draw an irregular shape, click and drag to draw the first line of the polygon, click again and drag to draw the next, and so on. When drawing the very last line, make sure you draw all the way to the start of your first line (closing the shape), and then release the mouse button.

✅ When you're done, it's okay if the hotpots don't perfectly match the regions and don't cover every bit of the picture. Just get them in the right ballpark.

✅ To change a hotspot's link, double-click the hotspot. To delete a hotspot, click it to select it, and then press the **Delete** key.

Using Borders, Backgrounds, Sounds, and Other Fun Stuff

In most Web pages, text carries the main content. Beyond the text, pictures often carry some of a page's true content. Even when they don't, they add pizazz, which helps attract and sustain visitor interest. Most Web pages contain nothing more than text, pictures, and links, so that's where this book has concentrated thus far.

Beyond those "Big Three" types of Web content, there is a motley assortment of other stuff you may or may not want to throw in, often just for kicks. You say you're a fan of miscellany? Lucky you—you're about to learn how to add backgrounds, picture borders, sounds, video, and other odds and ends to your pages.

FrontPage's **Themes** control some items you learn how to modify in this part, such as the background and text colors. If you are using a Theme for your page or Web and you want to change the background or colors, it's usually best to change these items by changing the Theme (choose **Format**, **Theme**), rather than changing these items individually in pages as described here.

Tasks

You can choose any color for a page's background, or you can use a picture for a background (see Task 2). While choosing a background color, it's smart to consider choosing text colors at the same time to ensure that the text colors are a good contrast to the background. (Text in a color that's too close to the background color is difficult to see.)

✓ If you've assigned a theme to this page, instead of doing this task, change background and text colors from the Themes dialog box (see Part 2).

✓ To copy the background and text colors from another page, click the **Get Background Information from Another Page** option at the bottom of the **Background** tab. Then click the **Browse** button next to that option and use the dialog box that appears to choose the page whose colors you want to use.

Task 1: Choosing Background and Text Colors

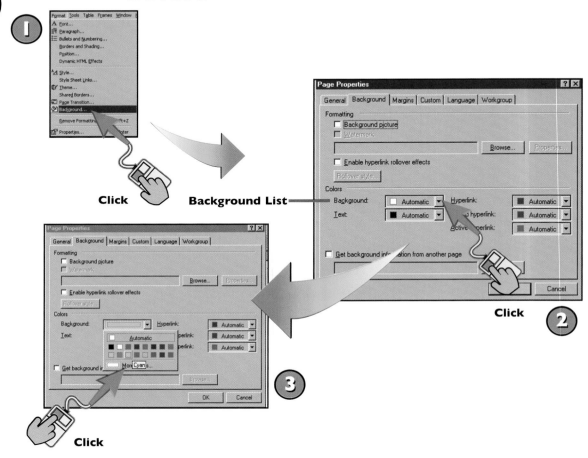

Start Here

Click

Background List

Click

Click

1 Choose **Format**, and then choose **Background**.

2 Click the **arrow** on the right side of the **Background** list box to open the list.

3 Click the colored square containing the color you want to use (or click **More Colors** to choose from a palette that offers a wider selection).

Next Step

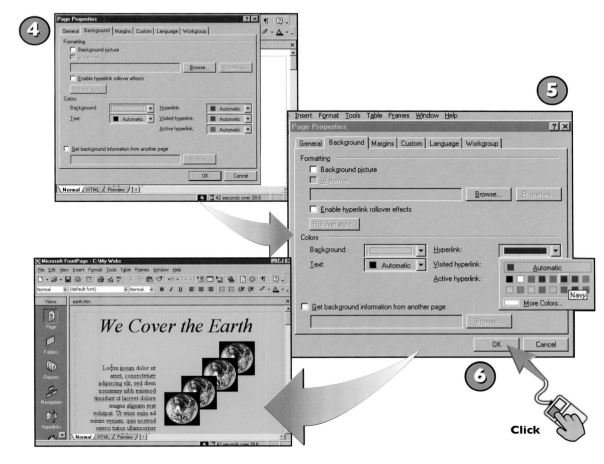

④ Observe the colored squares in the Text box and the three Hyperlink boxes, and consider whether they contrast well with the background color (and each other).

⑤ Use the list boxes to change text colors as necessary.

⑥ Click **OK**.

Click

✓ After choosing the default color for each kind of text, you can still assign any color you want to selected text by clicking the **Font Color** button on the **Formatting** toolbar.

✓ Users can configure their browsers to reject "custom" text and background colors you choose here and show the same colors for all pages instead. Users who do this (and they're few) will not see the text colors you choose, but will see the text itself just fine.

End Task

Task 2: Using a Picture Background

Instead of using a solid color background, as you learned to do in Task 1, you can use a picture as a background. If the picture is too small to fill the whole window in which the page appears, it is automatically *tiled*—repeated over and over—to fill the window. Tiling enables you to build a great-looking pattern out of the repeated image.

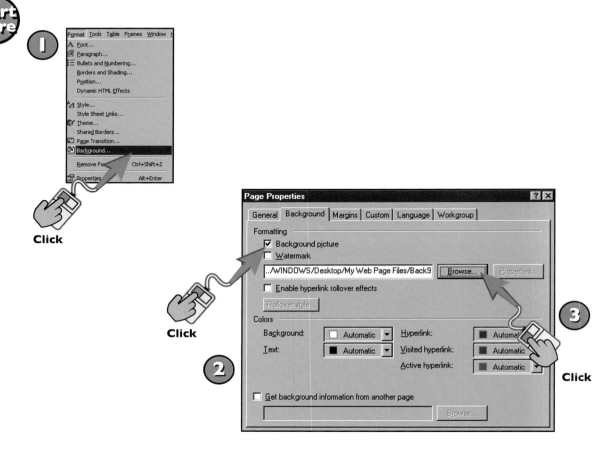

Start Here

Click

Click

Click

(✓) An image background automatically supersedes a background color. If you create an image background, any selection you may have made for background color is irrelevant.

① Choose **Format**, and then choose **Background**.

② Click the **Background Picture** check box to place a check mark there.

③ Click **Browse**.

Next Step

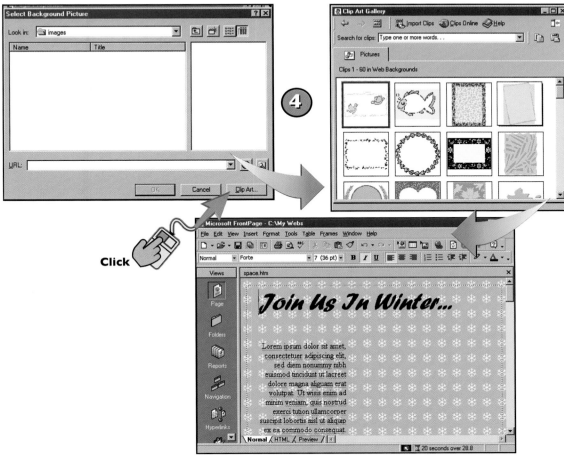

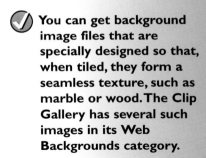

Click

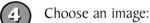

4 Choose an image:

If you have a GIF image you want to use for the background, use the dialog box to navigate to it, select it, and then click **OK**.

To choose a background from the Clip Gallery, click the **Clip Art** button, choose and insert a clip, close the Clip Gallery, and then click **OK** in the **Select Background Picture** dialog box.

✓ You can get background image files that are specially designed so that, when tiled, they form a seamless texture, such as marble or wood. The Clip Gallery has several such images in its **Web Backgrounds** category.

✓ An image background, like any picture file, slows the downloading of your page to the visitor, so watch out for using very large background files. Note that a large background image slows down the page much worse than a small picture tiled many times.

Sometimes, you can make certain pictures look a little classier by putting a nice box border around them. Here's how:

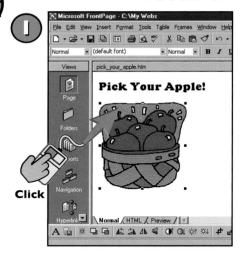

Task 3: Putting a Border Around a Picture

Start Here

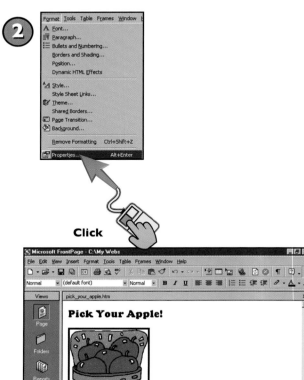

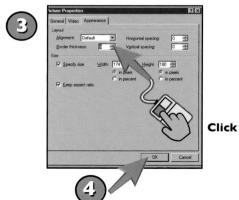

(✓) In step 3, a border thickness of I adds a very thin border, while 5 or higher adds a thick one. A border of 2, 3, or 4 usually looks best.

(✓) You can choose from an expanded selection of border options by selecting the picture, choosing **Format,** and then choosing **Borders and Shading.**

1 Click the picture to select it.

2 Choose **Format**, and then choose **Properties**.

3 In the **Border Thickness** box, type a number or click the up or down arrows for the thickness of the border you want. (A higher number makes a thicker border.)

4 Click **OK**.

End Task

Task 4: Adding a Bevel

Start Here

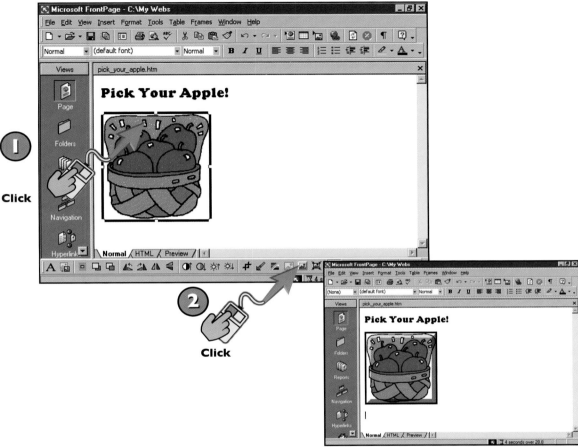

You can add a 3D effect to a picture's border by adding a *bevel*, a gray shadow along the bottom and right side. A bevel creates the illusion that the picture is floating above the page. It's a nice touch, if not overused.

Click

Click

① Click the picture to select it.

② Click the **Bevel** button on the Picture toolbar.

✓ You can add a bevel to a picture that has its own built-in border, or to any square or rectangular picture. The bevel really has nothing to do with the border; but since the bevel appears on only two sides, a bevel without some sort of apparent border on the other two sides looks a little funky.

Task 5: Organizing Pages with Horizontal Lines

Horizontal lines help divide up a page visually. Used between a heading and the paragraph that follows it, a line can add a little extra style to page. Lines also help divide sections of a longer page. Best of all, they're incredible easy to add, and they add graphical flair without slowing the download of the page in the way that pictures can.

Online, you'll see all sorts of fancy multicolor lines dividing up pages. These aren't real horizontal lines; they're pictures, used like lines, and you insert them like any other picture. You can find a great selection of these in Clip Gallery's Web Dividers category.

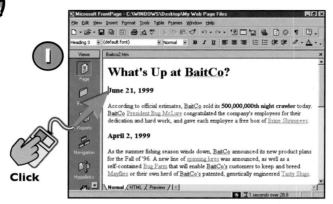

Click

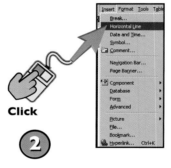

Click

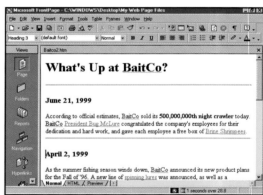

1. Click in your page at the spot where you want to insert the line.

2. Click **Insert**, and then choose **Horizontal Line**.

End Task

Task 6: Changing the Look of a Line

Start Here

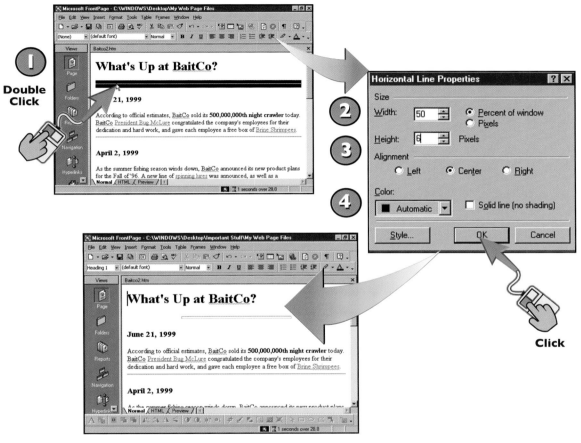

Double Click

Adding a basic horizontal line is a snap. But with just a little extra effort, you can change that line's appearance, making it thicker or thinner, making it shorter, and choosing its alignment and color.

Click

(1) Double-click a line you've inserted.

(2) To make the line shorter than the full width of the page, type a **Width** less than 100.

(3) Type a number in **Height** to change the thickness of the line; a higher number makes a thicker line.

(4) Choose an **Alignment** and **Color** for the line, and then click **OK**.

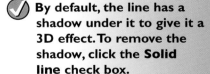

✓ By default, the line has a shadow under it to give it a 3D effect. To remove the shadow, click the **Solid line** check box.

End Task

Task 7: Playing a Background Sound

For a nice touch, you can make a sound effect or music clip play the moment a visitor arrives at the page. Only users of Internet Explorer 3 or later will hear the clip, so don't make the clip an essential part of understanding your page. Consider it a nice "throw-in" for the IE crowd.

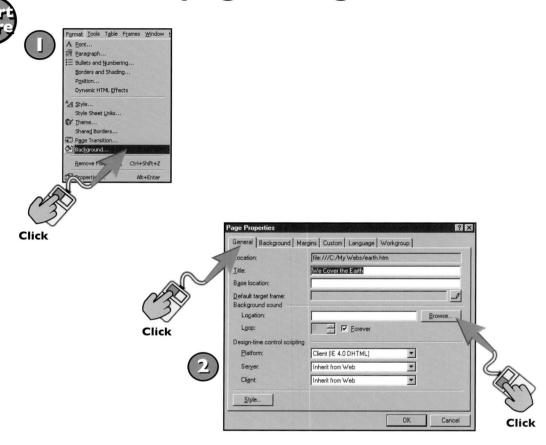

Start Here

Click

Click

Click

1 Choose **Format**, **Background**.

2 Click the **General** tab, and then click **Browse**.

Next Step

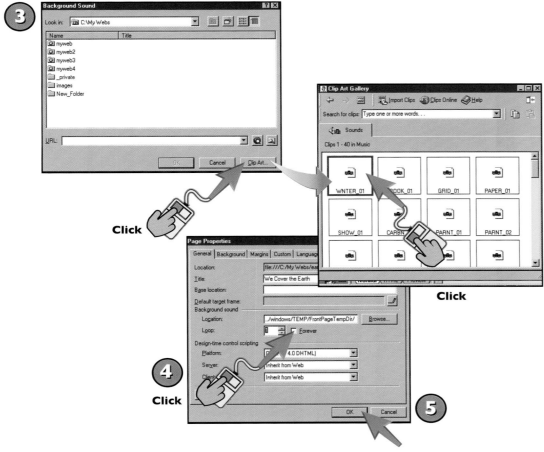

Click

Click

Click

3 To choose a sound clip, navigate to a sound clip file and select it, or click the **Clip Art** button, and choose and insert a sound clip.

4 In **Loop** options, check **Forever** to make the clip play over and over for as long as the visitor views the page, or type the number of times to play the sound in **Loop**.

5 Click **OK**.

✓ Sounds don't play in the Normal tab; to hear the background sound, preview the page.

✓ By connecting a microphone or other audio source (such as a cassette player) to your PC's sound card, you can record your own sound clips using Windows's built-in recorder.

Task 8: Adding Animation from the Clip Gallery

A special kind of GIF image file, called an *animated GIF*, plays a brief, simple animation when you view it in a Web page. You'll find animated GIFs in clip art libraries online and on disk, and you can create them with programs such as Microsoft's PhotoDraw. You'll find a bunch in FrontPage's clip art library, where they're called *motion clips*. Go figure.

✔ To search for clips matching a keyword, enter the keyword as shown in Part 6, "Adding and Formatting Pictures." All of the items shown on the Motion Clips tab will be matches for that keyword.

✔ To find animated GIF clip art sites, search with Yahoo (www.yahoo.com) or another search page by using animated gif as a search term. Download the clip and insert it in a page exactly as you would any GIF from online (see Part 6), and then preview the page to see the animation.

Click

Click

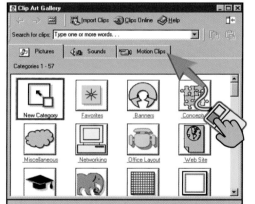

Click

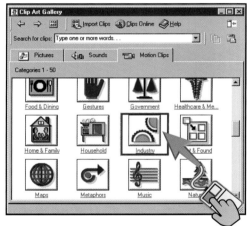

Click

1 Click in your page at the general spot where you want to insert the animation.

2 Click **Insert,** choose **Picture**, and then choose **Clip Art.**

3 Click the **Motion Clips** tab.

4 Scroll through the categories listed, and click a likely looking category to display still-image thumbnails of the available clips.

Next Step

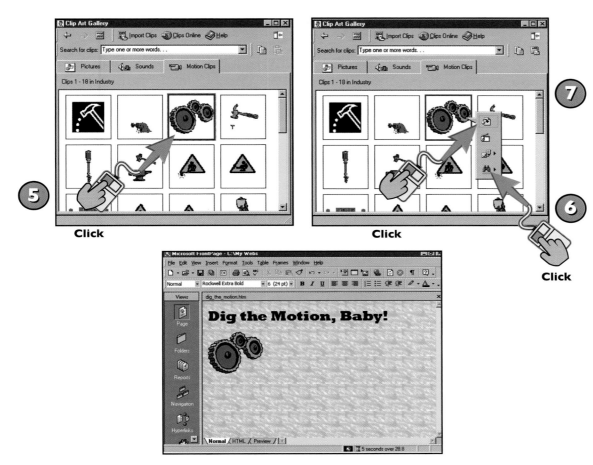

Click

Click

Click

(5) Scroll through the clips shown, and when you see one you like, click it once.

(6) To see the animation play before you insert it click the **Play Clip** button.

(7) Click **Insert Clip** to insert the clip in your Web page and then click the **X** button in Clip Gallery's upper-right corner.

✓ Note that your animation won't play in the Normal tab; to see the animation play in your page, preview the page.

✓ You change the size, shape, position, and other aspects of an animated GIF exactly as you would a regular GIF (see Part 6) .

End Task

Task 9: Using Graphical Bullets

In many bulleted lists you'll see online, the bullets are not symbol characters, but little pictures—stars, suns, smiles, and so on. These "graphical bullets" are pretty easy to apply, and FrontPage's clip library even includes a hefty collection of choices (check out the Web Bullets category). But you can use any picture as a bullet, as long as you reduce it to bullet-size proportions.

✓ You can also add graphical bullets by choosing a theme (see Part 2). If you choose a theme, graphical bullets will be applied automatically to any list you format with the Bullets button.

✓ If you use small animated GIFs for bullets, you'll have animated bullets. Isn't that nice?

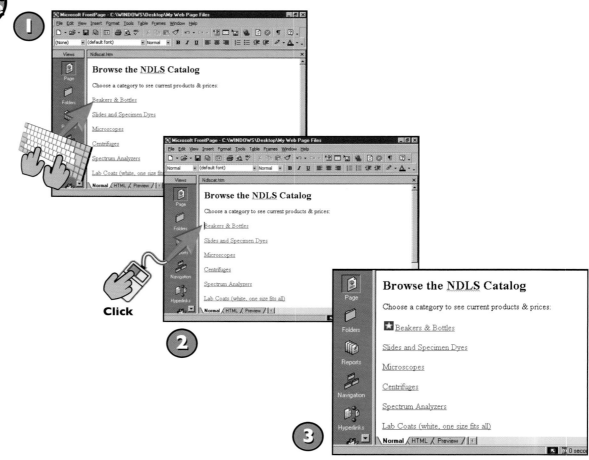

Start Here

Click

① Type the list items as ordinary paragraphs, pressing **Enter** after each. (**Do not** click the Bullets button!)

② Click to the left of the first item.

③ Insert the picture file you'll use as a bullet, any way you like (from a file, from Clip Gallery, by scanning; see Part 6).

Next Step ▶

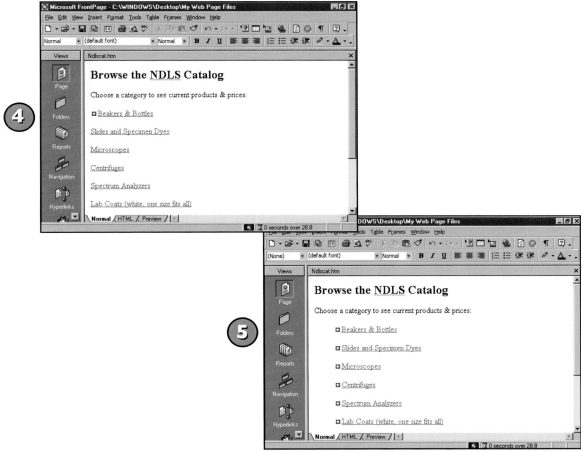

To use a different bullet picture on each item, repeat steps 2–4 for each item.

To indent the finished list (after adding the bullets), click and hold to the left of the bullet on the first item, drag downward to select the whole list—*including* all bullets—and then click the **Increase Indent** button.

To increase the space between the picture and the text, right-click the picture, choose **Image Properties,** and then click the **Appearance** tab. Increase the number in **Horizontal Spacing,** and then click **OK.**

④ Format the bullet picture as desired (size, shape, and so on) .

⑤ Select the bullet, and click the **Copy** button. Click to the left of the second list item, and then click **Paste**. For remaining items, click to the left of the item, and click **Paste**.

Task 10: Inserting a Video Clip

With a video capture card installed in your PC and a video source (such as a camcorder or VCR), you can create video files in Windows Video (.AVI) format. FrontPage makes inserting those clips in your pages easy and presents them attractively as frozen, still pictures in the page that play automatically or at the visitor's option.

FrontPage's method of showing the clip "inline" like a picture is viewable only through Internet Explorer 3 or later, and may degrade the performance of the page. Use this task only when the page will be published on an intranet. For the Web, it's better to put a link in the page that the visitor can click to download the video file and play it outside the page (see Part 5, "Making Hyperlinks").

Click

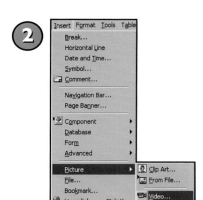

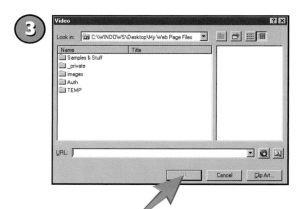

Click

① Click in your page at the general spot where you want the video clip to appear.

② Click **Insert,** choose **Picture**, and then choose **Video.**

③ Navigate to and select the AVI file, and then click **OK** to insert it in the page.

④ Right-click the picture, and choose **Picture Properties**.

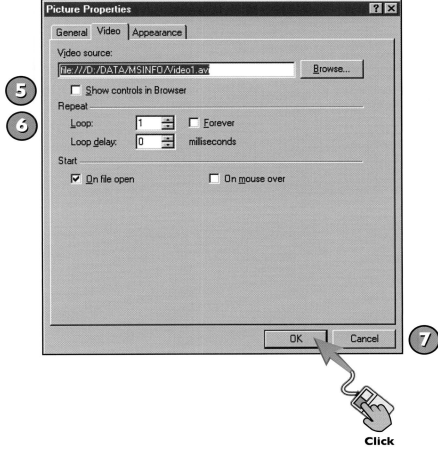

Click

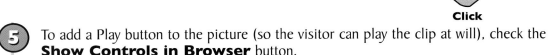

⑤ To add a Play button to the picture (so the visitor can play the clip at will), check the **Show Controls in Browser** button.

⑥ To play automatically and continuously, check the **Forever** check box. To play automatically a set number of times, type the number of times to play in **Loop**.

⑦ Click **OK**.

✓ When the clip will be played repeatedly (*looped*) a set number of times or forever, you can add a brief pause between each loop by entering a number in **Loop Delay**. The delay is measured in milliseconds (1/1000ths of a second), so a Loop Delay of 500 adds a half-second pause.

✓ Video doesn't play in the Normal tab; to see the video play in your page, preview the page.

End Task

Creating Tables

Web pages offer lots of tools for organizing content in attractive ways: headings, lists, indentation, alignment, horizontal lines, and wrapping around pictures. But when you have a lot of stuff—eight or more items—that fall logically into groups, a nice table is the way to go.

Even when your content isn't "tabular" in nature, you'll find tables come in handy in another way. You can use a big table to design and control the layout of a whole page (as some of FrontPage's templates do).

In this part, you discover how easy it is to make tables in FrontPage 2000, and to make them look great.

Task

Task 1: Inserting a Really Fast New Table

All you need to get started with tables is a page in progress, a rough idea of what you want to put in the table (sometimes it helps to scribble the table longhand first, to plan the table), and a rough idea of where you want to put it. Then you take off. Here's the quickest way to start a table.

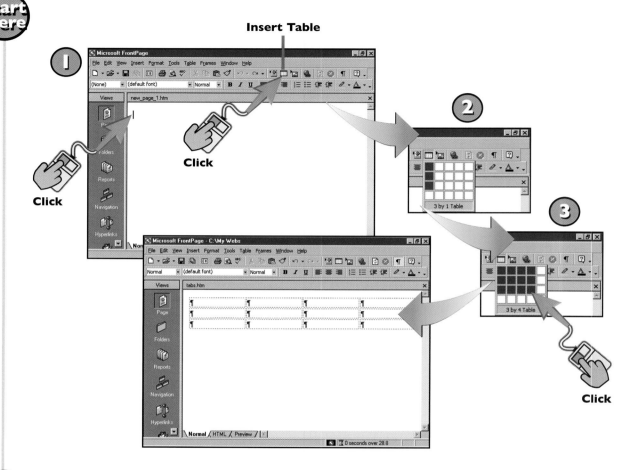

Insert Table

Start Here

Click

Click

3 by 1 Table

3 by 4 Table

Click

✓ The dashed lines that show the table borders and gridlines in the Normal tab just show where your table is—they won't show up when you preview the page. That's OK—a table without borders can look pretty cool. But if you really *want* visible borders, see Task 9.

✓ Don't worry about the size (or number) of the rows and columns in the table right after you insert it. As you put content into the table, the rows and columns will expand to fit that content.

1 Click the **Insert Table** button on the **Standard** toolbar.

2 Move the mouse downward (don't click or hold!) to highlight the number of rows you want.

3 Move the mouse to the right to highlight the number of columns you want, and then click.

End Task

Task 2: Inserting a New Table

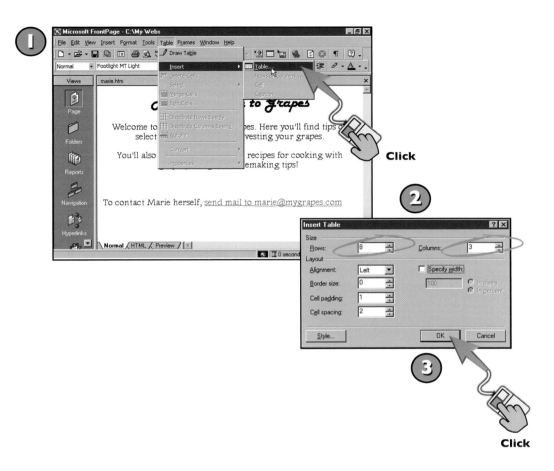

Click

Click

When the table will be bigger than 4×5, or when you want to select certain formatting options while creating the table, FrontPage offers table-creation Method 2.

(1) Choose **Table,** choose **Insert**, and then choose **Table**.

(2) In **Rows** and **Columns**, choose the number of rows and columns for the table.

(3) Click **OK**.

Any of the options on the Insert Table dialog box—width (the fix width of the table), border, alignment, and padding—can also be selected or changed later, after you create the table. You'll learn about all of these options later in this part.

If you have another Windows program in which you can create tables, such as Microsoft Word or a spreadsheet program such as Excel, you can create tables there and then import those tables right into your FrontPage pages. This not only enables you to create tables by using programs you already know, but also to easily reuse tables you may already have in word processing or spreadsheet documents.

Task 3: Importing a Table from Another Program

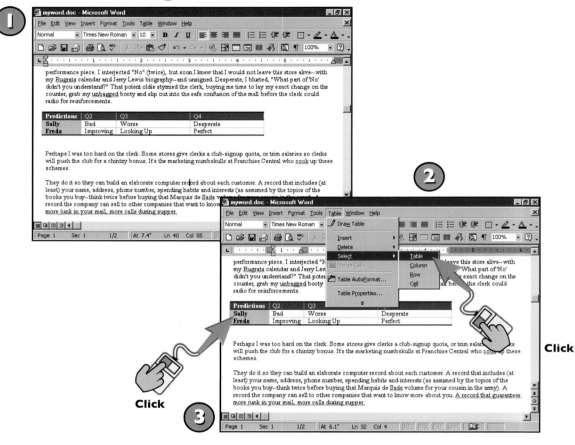

Start Here

Click

Click

Click

In most programs, instead of step 3, you can click a Copy button on the toolbar, or choose Edit, Copy. But in case those options aren't available, Ctrl+Ins always works in Windows programs.

1. In the other program, open the file containing the table (or create the table).

2. Select the table. In Word, click the table and choose **Table**, **Select**, **Table**. In Excel, highlight the portion of the current worksheet you want to import.

3. Press and hold the **Ctrl** key, press the **Insert** key, and then release.

Next Step

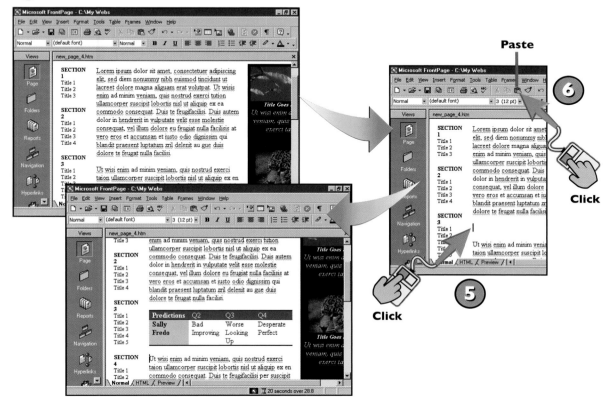

Paste

Click

Click

4 Switch to (or open) the FrontPage file.

5 Click the spot where you want the table to go.

6 Click the **Paste** button on the **Standard** toolbar.

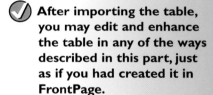

✓ After importing the table, you may edit and enhance the table in any of the ways described in this part, just as if you had created it in FrontPage.

End Task

Task 4: Deleting a Table

The Web author who createth hath the power to taketh away. (Or something like that.) Here's how to kill a table.

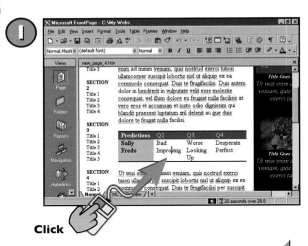

Start Here

1

Click

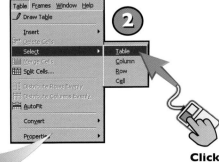

2

Click

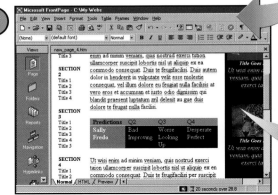

3

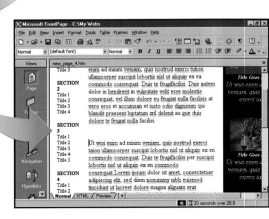

✓ To move a table, perform steps 1 and 2, and then click and hold on the selected table, drag where you want it, and release.

✓ To copy a table, perform steps 1 and 2, click the Copy button, click in the page where you want the copy, and then click Paste.

1 Click anywhere in the table.

2 Choose **Table**, **Select**, and then choose **Table**.

3 Press the **Delete** key.

End Task

Task 5: Putting Text in Table Cells

Start Here

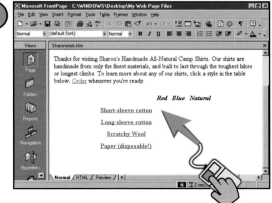

Click

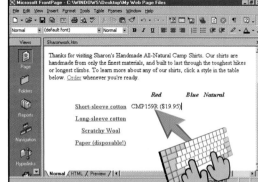

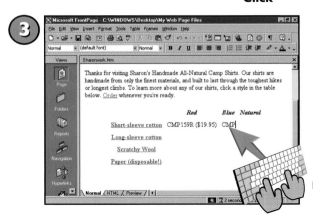

Tab

A table without content is like walls without furniture. Here's how to start filling in your new table by putting text in *cells*—the boxes formed by each intersection of a row and column.

(✓) You can apply to text in a table any of the character formatting from Part 4, "Saying It with Style," including fonts, sizes, bold, italic, underlining, or color. Making the text in all cells of the top row bold, italic, or a unique color is a nice way to create column headings that stand out.

(✓) If you apply alignment (see Part 4) to text in a cell, the text is aligned relative to the cell it's in, not the page. For example, if you apply center alignment to text in a cell, the text is centered within the cell.

1. Click in the cell in which you want to add text.

2. Type whatever you want.

3. Press the **Tab** key to jump to the next cell (or click in the cell you want to fill next).

Task 6: Putting Pictures in a Table

Most tables are mostly text. But you can give your table panache by using a picture or two in its cells.

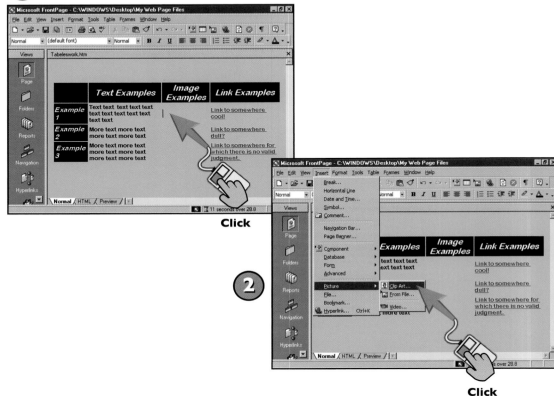

Click

Click

✓ Yes, you *can* put an animated **GIF** picture in a table cell.

✓ You can put links in a table, too. Just add to the table the text or picture you want to use as the link source, highlight that text or picture in its table cell, and create the link as usual (see Part 5, "Making Hyperlinks").

① Click in the cell in which you want to put a picture.

② Using any of the techniques from Part 6, "Adding and Formatting Pictures" (Insert Clip Art, Insert Picture, scan, and so on), insert the picture.

Next Step

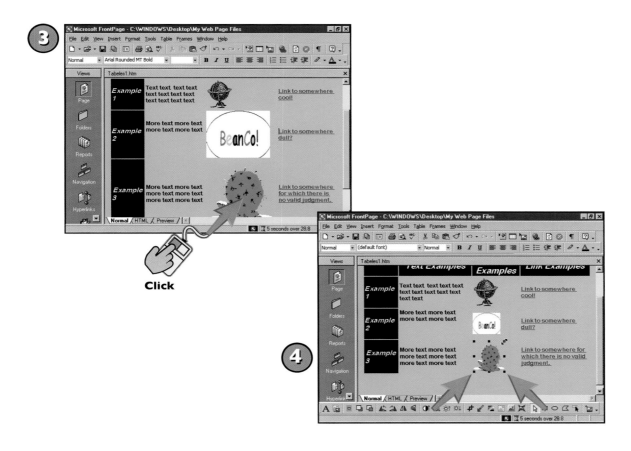

Click

③ Continue adding pictures to cells until you've added all the pictures for this table.

④ On each picture, drag a corner handle (see Part 6) to scale the picture to the size you desire.

✓ **When you have sized all of the pictures, the row and column sizes will have changed their size to match.**

✓ **You can use any of the picture formatting techniques from Part 6 on a picture in a table cell. To open the Image Properties dialog box to format a picture in a cell, point to the picture, right-click, and choose Picture Properties from the pop-up menu.**

End Task

Task 7: Using a Big Table to Design a Page

By creating a table so big that it covers the whole page, you give yourself the ability to put each chunk of page content—a paragraph here, a picture there—in its own cell. That enables you to arrange text and pictures in ways that would otherwise be impossible (unless you opted for "absolute positioning" and the limitations that come with it).

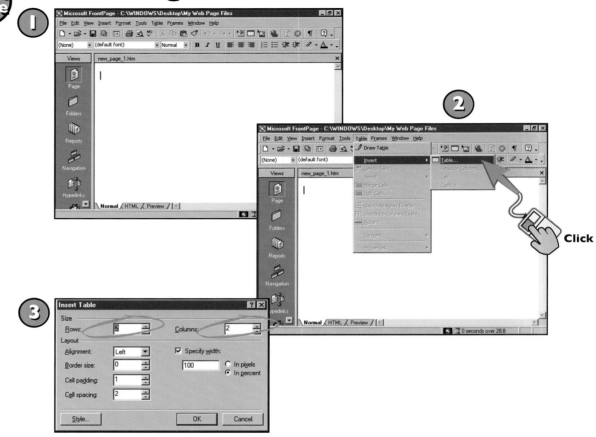

Click

✓ Most of the pages you create from templates are formatted by big tables. Use the table editing steps from Tasks 12-14 to change the layout of pages you create from templates.

① Start with a new blank page.

② Click **Table**, choose **Insert**, and then choose **Table**.

③ In **Rows** and **Columns**, choose the number of rows and columns for the table.

Next Step

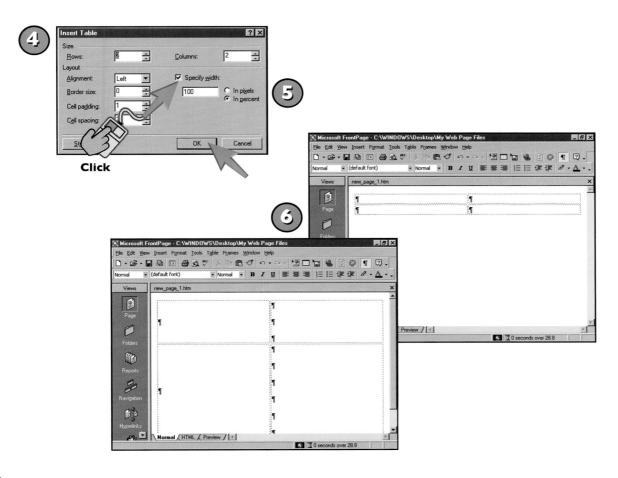

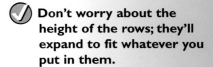

④ Click **Specify Width** to insert a check mark in the check box.

⑤ Make sure the number in the box is **100**, and the **in Percent** option is selected, to create a table that is 100% the width of the page. Click **OK**.

⑥ Create your content in the cells.

Don't worry about the height of the rows; they'll expand to fit whatever you put in them.

Task 8: Adding a Caption to a Table

Some tables need a *caption*—a descriptive title directly above or below the cells—and some don't. For your own tables, you get to choose.

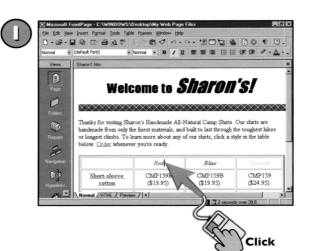

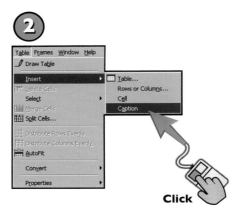

Click

Click

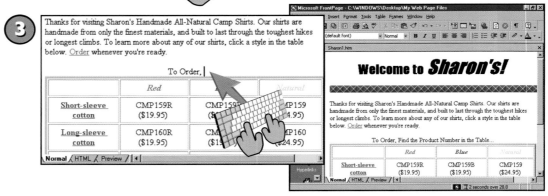

✓ To format the text of the caption, double-click the caption to select it, and then apply formatting— font, size, color, and so on.

✓ FrontPage automatically puts captions above the table, but you can move a caption below the table. Click anywhere on the caption, click Table, choose Properties, and then choose Caption. A dialog box appears, giving you two choices for caption placement: Top of Table and Bottom of Table.

1 Click anywhere in the table whose caption you want to add.

2 Click **Table**, choose **Insert,** and then choose **Caption**.

3 Type your caption.

Task 9: Dressing Up Tables with Borders

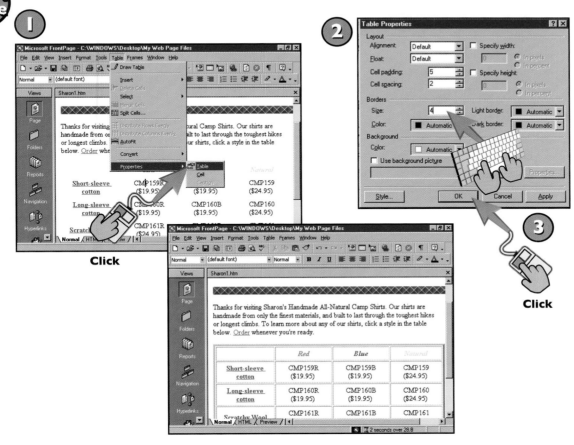

Click

Click

So far, your table does a great job of lining up its content in rows and columns, but it lacks the nice grid of lines—and box all around—that delineate the content and make the table look sharp.

✓ In step 2, the higher the number, the thicker the border. A 4 in Size creates a nice, moderately heavy border; I creates an elegant, thin border.

✓ In the Table Properties dialog box, the box below Border Size—Cell Padding—lets you adjust the spacing between the contents of a cell and the walls around that cell. Raising the number in Cell Padding to, say, 3 or 4, creates more space around the cell contents, making the cell seem less crowded.

① Click anywhere in the table, click **Table**, choose **Properties**, and then choose **Table**.

② Under **Borders**, click in the **Size** box and type a number for the width of the borders.

③ Click **OK**.

End Task

Task 10: Choosing Custom Border Colors

A table border is not one line, but three lines used together to create a 3D effect: a basic border line, a "light border" (a highlight on the top of horizontal lines and on the left side of vertical lines) and a "dark border" (a shadow on the bottom of horizontal lines and on the right side of vertical lines). You can pick the color for each part of the border.

✓ To experiment with borders, border colors, and anything else in the Table Properties dialog box, make any changes in the dialog box, and then click the Apply button instead of OK. The changes are made in the table, but the Table Properties dialog box remains open, so you can try different settings.

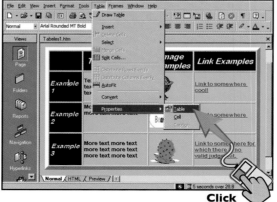

Click

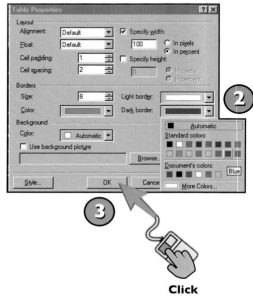

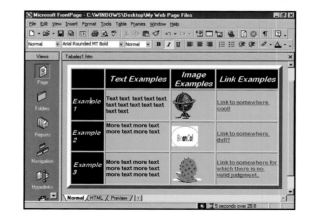

Click

1. Click anywhere in the table, click **Table**, choose **Properties**, and then choose **Table**.

2. In the **Borders** section, choose a color from each of the three lists: **Color**, **Light Border**, and **Dark Border**.

3. Click **OK**.

Task 11: Choosing a Background for a Table

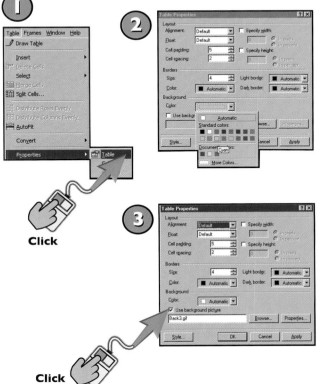

Click

Click

Unless you add a background to a table, the page's background color or image shows through the table (but does not obscure the table's content or borders). But a table can have its own background, different from that of the page, to make the table—and more important, its contents—really stand out.

✓ If you choose both a background image and a background color, the color is irrelevant—a background image overrides a background color.

✓ You can use a different background for a selected cell or cells than for the rest of the table; for example, you can give the top row its own unique background to make column headings stand out. In step 1, click in a cell, click Table, and then choose Select Cell, Select Row, or Select Column.

① Click anywhere in the table, click **Table**, choose **Properties**, and then choose **Table**.

② To add a solid color background, open the **Color** list under **Background** and choose a color.

③ To add a picture background, click the check box next to **Use background picture**. Then type the name of the picture file to use, or **Browse** for it.

Task 12: Adding New Rows

*Ooops….*The table needs another row. **No need to start over; just add what you need to the bottom of the table.**

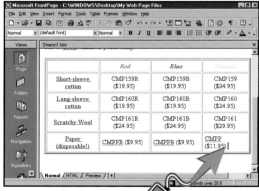

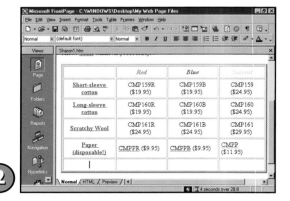

Click

✓ **To insert a new row, but not at the bottom, click in any cell in the row you want to be directly *above* the new row. Choose Table, Insert, Row or Columns, and then click OK on the dialog box.**

① In the bottom row, click in the cell farthest to the right.

② Press the **Tab** key to create a new row.

③ To add even more rows, keep pressing **Tab**.

Task 13: Adding New Columns

Start Here

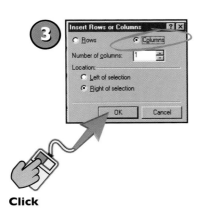

Click

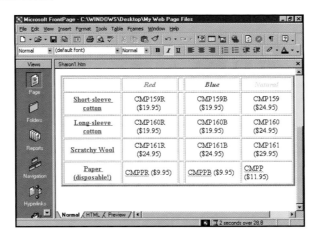

Click

Click

Ooops, redux! **Now the table needs another** *column.* **That's what you get for not planning ahead. But no problem.**

✅ **To add more than one column to the right of the selected column, change the Number of Columns in the Insert Rows or Columns dialog box.**

✅ **If you want the new column to be the leftmost column, click in the column that's farthest left now, perform steps 2 and 3, click the Left of Selection option, and then click OK.**

1. Click in any cell in the column that will be the one to the left of the new column.

2. Choose **Table**, **Insert**, **Rows or Columns**.

3. Choose the **Columns** option, and click **OK**.

Task 14: Fine-Tuning Row and Column Sizes

After inserting all of your content, you may want to fine-tune the width of columns or height of rows, especially when you're using a table to control page layout (see Part 7, "Using Borders, Backgrounds, Sounds, and Other Fun Stuff"). You can do this simply by dragging the space between two rows or columns.

Start Here

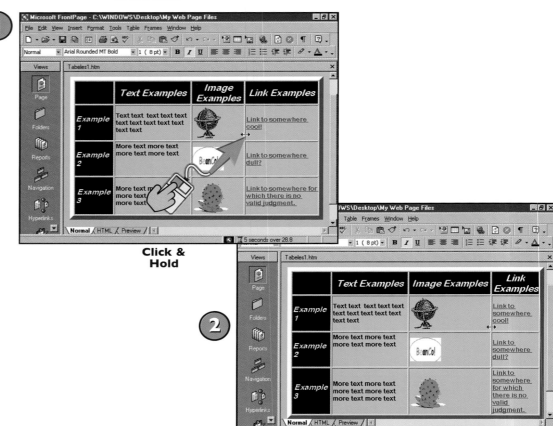

Click & Hold

To make all rows or all columns all the same size (for regularity), regardless of their contents, choose Table, and then choose Distribute Rows Evenly or Distribute Columns Evenly.

If you're not happy with your fine-tuning, you can make the table revert to basing its row heights and column widths on the size of cell contents by clicking anywhere in the table and choosing Table, Autofit.

1 Point carefully to the space between rows or columns until you see the pointer become a two-sided arrow. Click and hold.

2 Drag the line to where you want it, and then release the mouse button.

End Task

Task 15: Aligning a Table on the Page

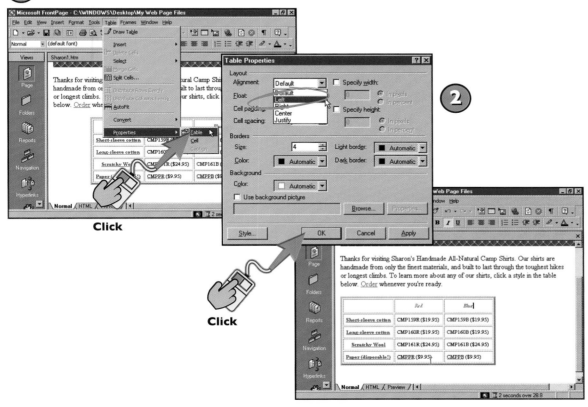

Click

Click

When a table is less than 100 percent of the width of the page, you can align it in the same positions you can align a paragraph or picture: left, center, or right. However, the usual alignment buttons don't do the job for tables. Here's the deal:

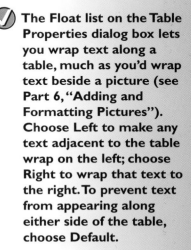

The Float list on the Table Properties dialog box lets you wrap text along a table, much as you'd wrap text beside a picture (see Part 6, "Adding and Formatting Pictures"). Choose Left to make any text adjacent to the table wrap on the left; choose Right to wrap that text to the right. To prevent text from appearing along either side of the table, choose Default.

1 Click anywhere in the table, click **Table**, choose **Properties**, and then choose **Table**.

2 Open the **Alignment** list, and choose **Left**, **Center**, or **Right**. Click **OK**.

PART 9

Building a Web

What's a web? Well, "web" is FrontPage's way of describing a group of pages designed to work together as a cohesive Web site.

In FrontPage, you can easily create a set of pages, insert hyperlinks in each that lead to the other pages, and publish them as a site—you needn't fuss with FrontPage's webs. However, creating webs has its advantages. When you apply a theme, you'll have the option to add the theme to the whole web, giving the pages a consistent appearance and avoiding the effort of changing them one by one. When you run spell check, you'll see an option to check all pages in the web at once. When you publish… You get the idea.

Best of all, a web enables you to add FrontPage *navigation bars*, rows of buttons or text links that lead to other pages in the web. When you use navigation bars, you don't need to create the hyperlinks behind them—that's automatic. And when you change a page's title, the navigation bar buttons leading to that page from other pages change automatically to the new title.

Webs aren't essential. But they can save you a lot of time.

Tasks

The quickest and easiest way to kick off a new web is to pick a wizard. The wizard will build a rough web (built on a template) that shows the general organization and feel you'll want for your own. You can then edit that web in any way you wish to make it your own.

Task 1: Starting a New Web with a Wizard

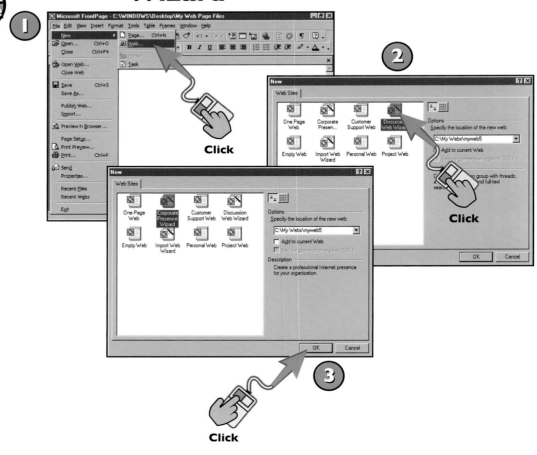

Click

Click

Click

✓ Between steps 2 and 3, you can enter a disk location in the Location box to choose where the new web will be saved. That'll save you time when you save the web later.

✓ Whenever you use a wizard to create a web, study all of the pages in it before making changes. Each page contains instructions and tips you may find useful.

① Click **File**, **New**, and then choose **Web**.

② **Click** each of the Wizard icons (the ones with magic wands) in the Web sites tab, and read the description that appears on the right side of the dialog box.

③ When the description shown is the best match for the web you want to create, click **OK**.

Next Step

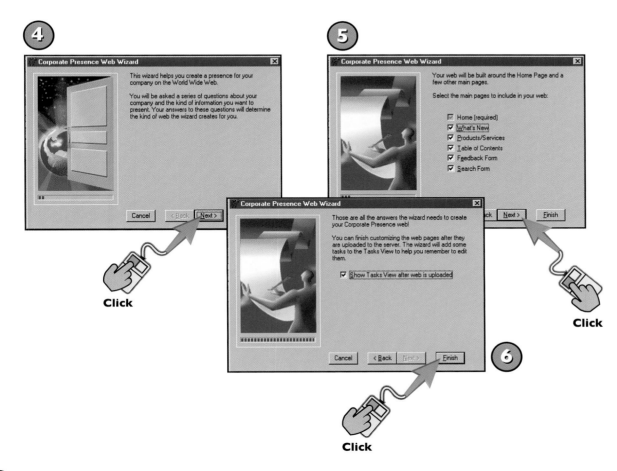

4 Read the Welcome message, and then click **Next**.

5 Work through the pages presented to you, making any changes you wish, and click **Next** when you're done with each.

6 On the final page (where the Next button will no longer work), click **Finish**.

✓ You needn't make changes to every page the wizard shows you. On any one, you can simply click Next to accept the choices shown and move on.

✓ Along the way, you may be presented with a button you can click to choose a theme to be applied to all pages in your web (see Part 2 for more about themes). If you don't choose a theme in the Wizard, you can always choose one later by choosing Format, Theme.

Task 2: Previewing Your Web

Right after you create a web with a wizard, you may find yourself in Tasks view. Tasks are really only important for dividing work among multiple authors creating a site together. For now, you need to switch to Navigation view, which displays the pages in the web in a tree diagram, to help you understand (and edit) the way the site is organized.

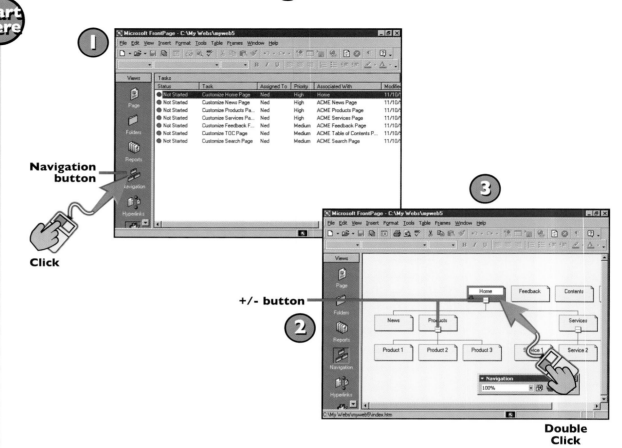

Navigation button

Click

+/- button

Double Click

✓ The apparent relationships among pages in the tree do not necessarily reflect the way pages are linked together. However, these relationships are important, because they can determine which pages the navigation bar on a given page points to (see Tasks 8–10).

1 In the **Views** bar, click the **Navigation** button.

2 To show or hide the page icons in branches of the tree, click the **plus or minus** icons.

3 To view and edit any page in the web in Page view, double-click its icon.

Task 3: Seeing All of the Tree

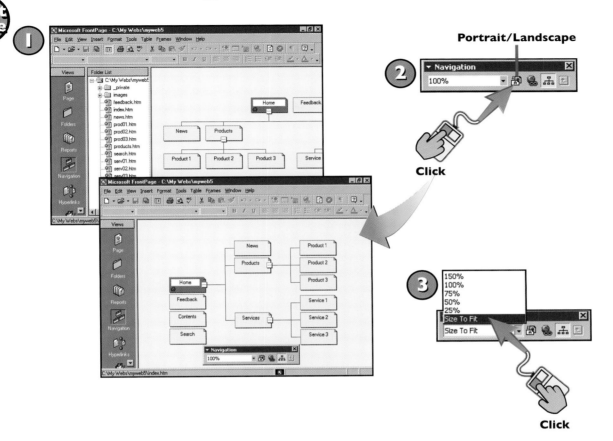

Start Here

Portrait/Landscape

Click

Click

With larger, more complex webs, you may not be able to see the whole tree diagram at once without scrolling. That's a problem, because you can't really assess the structure of your Web site unless you can view the whole tree. Here are ways to see more.

① If you see the folder list (which shows how the web and its pages are stored), hide it by choosing **View**, **Folder List**.

② On the Navigation toolbar, click the **Portrait/Landscape** button to change the presentation of the tree from horizontal to vertical, or vice versa.

③ If steps 1 and 2 don't do the job, open the list on the Navigation toolbar and choose **Size to Fit**.

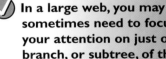 In a large web, you may sometimes need to focus your attention on just one branch, or subtree, of the web. To display only one subtree in Navigation view, click the icon at the top of the subtree you want to view, and then click the **View Subtree Only** button on the **Navigation toolbar**.

End Task

It's not necessary to save webs—changes to a web are saved automatically as you create and edit it. However, pages you change within the web must be saved. You can save pages as you work on them or just save when you close or exit, as shown in the following steps.

Task 4: Closing and Opening a Web

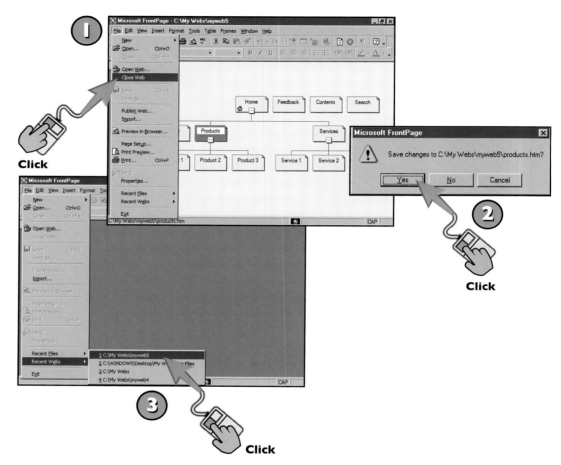

Start Here

Click

Click

Click

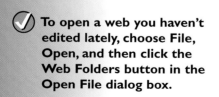
To open a web you haven't edited lately, choose File, Open, and then click the Web Folders button in the Open File dialog box.

① To close a web, choose **File,** and then choose **Close Web,** or simply exit FrontPage.

② If any pages in the web have been changed but not saved, a message appears, asking whether you want to save changes. Click **Yes** to save.

③ To open a web, choose **File,** choose **Recent Webs,** and then choose the web you want.

End Task

Task 5: Adding a Page to a Web

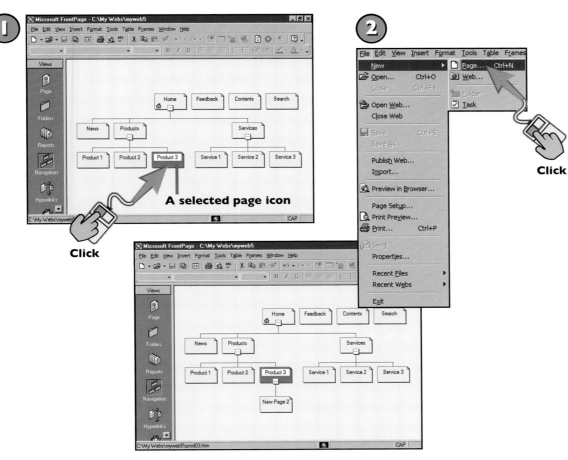

A selected page icon

Click

Click

2

Your web looks about right, but short a page or two. Before you start fiddling with individual pages, add the pages you need.

Click

① In Navigation view, click the page that will be directly above the new one in the tree.

② Choose **File**, **New**, and then choose **Page**.

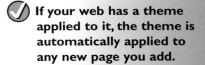
If your web has a theme applied to it, the theme is automatically applied to any new page you add.

Task 6: Deleting a Page from a Web

Did the wizard give you a more complex, expansive web than you need? Cut it down to what you want.

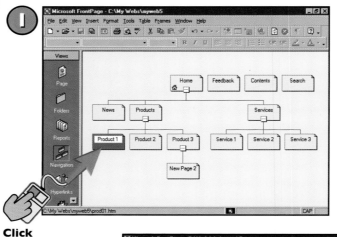

Click

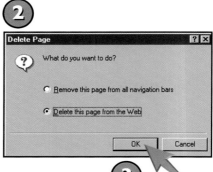

Click

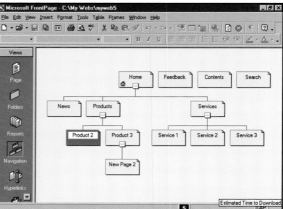

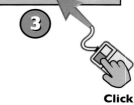

(✓) **If the page you delete has other pages under it, FrontPage asks in step 2 whether you want the page *and all pages below it* deleted or simply removed from all navigation bars.**

(1) In Navigation view, click the page you want to delete, and then press your **Delete** key.

(2) Choose whether to remove the page from the navigation bars of other pages in the web (but leave the page file in place) or to delete the page file altogether.

(3) Click **OK**.

Task 7: Moving a Page

Start Here

Maybe now your web has all the right pages, but not in the right organization. Here's how to re-organize.

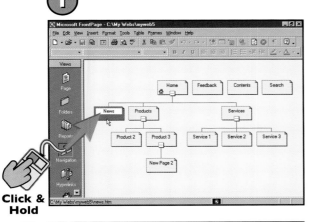

Click & Hold

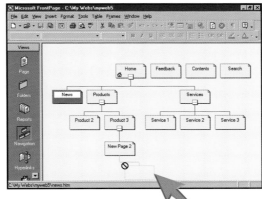

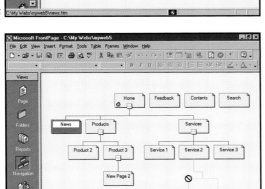

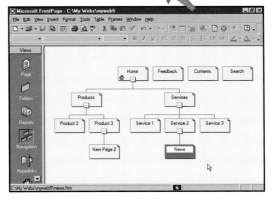

(1) Click and hold on a page you want to move.

(2) Drag the folder to where you want it to go, watching carefully for the line that appears to show how the two would relate if you released the button.

(3) When the line shows the relationship you want, release the mouse button.

 Anytime you add, delete, or move a page in a web, you can click the Undo button to reverse that action.

End Task

Task 8: Changing the Navigation Bar

Most web templates add a navigation bar automatically. (If you managed to create a web without one, and you want one, see Task 9.) Though you may want to keep the bar, you may prefer that any given page include a different set of buttons or show different formatting than what the template gives it. Here's how to change the bar on any page.

Start Here

Double Click

✓ If your site uses a theme (see Part 2), you can change the appearance of the navigation bar buttons by changing the theme.

✓ To delete a navigation bar, click it once to highlight it and then press the Delete key. Note that you remove the bar from one page at a time; you cannot remove it from a whole web in one shot.

1 Display the page whose navigation bar you want to modify in Page view's **Normal** tab.

2 Double-click the navigation bar.

3 Examine the diagram of the web and the key beneath it. As you make changes in the dialog box, the diagram shows the results.

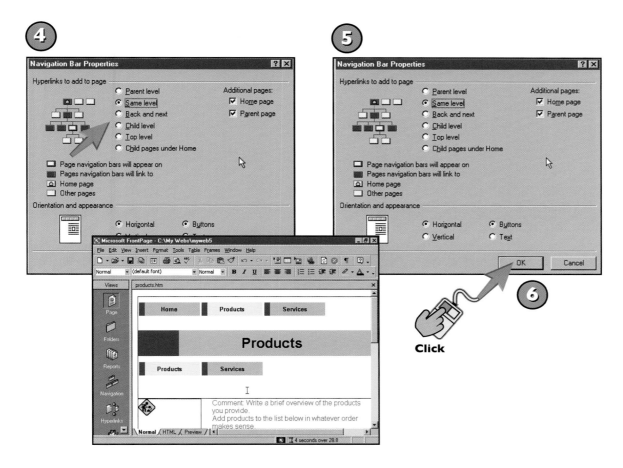

Choose which set of pages the bar should have links for, such as **Parent level** (the row directly above, in the same branch), or **Child level** (the row below).

Choose the bar's Orientation and appearance: as a **Horizontal** row or **Vertical** column, and as **Buttons** or as simple **Text** links.

Click **OK**.

✓ In a navigation bar, you can optionally add the web's home page or the page's parent page (the page directly above it in its subtree) by checking the check boxes provided.

✓ The Back and Next option does not link the navigation bar to specific pages. Instead, it creates a bar with two buttons which, when clicked, have exactly the same effect as clicking the browser's Back and Forward buttons.

Task 9: Adding a Navigation Bar

Most web templates add a navigation bar automatically. But if you don't have one for your web and want one, here's how to get it.

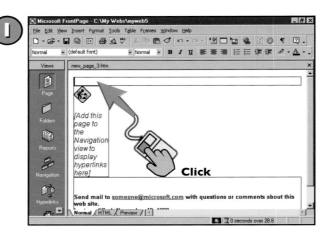

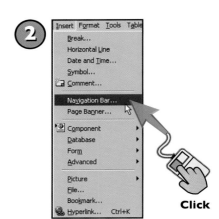

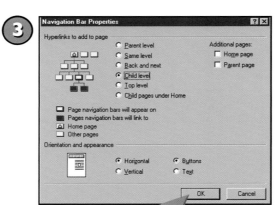

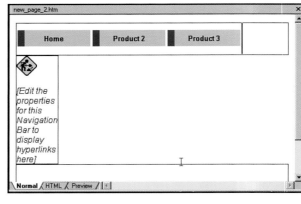

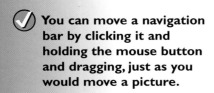
You can move a navigation bar by clicking it and holding the mouse button and dragging, just as you would move a picture.

Viewing the page in Page view's Normal tab, click where you want to insert the bar.

Choose **Insert**, and then choose **Navigation Bar**.

Choose from the options in the Navigation Bar Properties dialog box (as described in Task 8), and then click **OK**.

Task 10: Testing a Navigation Bar

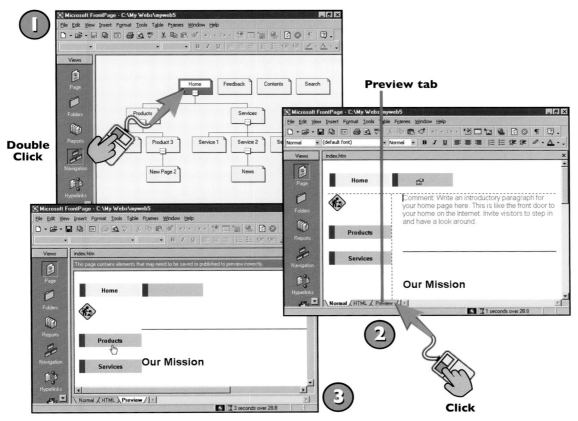

Double Click

Preview tab

Click

After your web is roughly organized and its pages contain the kind of navigation bars you want, you can test the flow of your site by testing the navigation buttons.

① Open the web in Navigation view, and double-click the very top page icon in the tree to open it in Page view.

② Click the **Preview** tab to preview the page.

③ Use the navigation bar on the top page to navigate to other pages, and use the bars on others to navigate throughout your web.

✔ Another way to study how your web holds together is to open its top page, and then click the Hyperlinks button on the Views bar. In the Hyperlinks view, you see where all the links on the top page lead. You also can click the + signs on the pages to display a diagram of where they lead.

PART 10

Adding Cool Effects

Most of the important cool stuff you can add to pages has been covered already, especially in Part 6, "Adding and Formatting Pictures," and Part 7, "Using Borders, Backgrounds, Sounds, and Other Fun Stuff." But there are a few other fun doodads FrontPage 2000 can add to your pages—at a price.

The cool stuff you can add by following steps in this part falls mostly into a category called *components*. In some cases, components in Web pages show up properly only when the page is viewed through Internet Explorer 4 or later, not through other browsers. (Which also means that you must have Internet Explorer 4 or later to preview your work!) In other cases, a component supports multiple browsers, but requires that special Microsoft software—called *FrontPage extensions*—be installed on the server where the page is published.

So although the stuff in this part is fun and easy to add, you should refrain from using it except in pages to be published on a local intranet where all users have Internet Explorer 4 or later or where you know that the FrontPage Extensions are on the server. On the Internet, too many of your potential visitors will be unable to see your masterpiece in its full glory.

Tasks

Task 1: Creating Hover Buttons

A *hover button* is a button whose appearance changes when a visitor points to it or even simply passes the pointer over it. The button may glow, change color, or even appear to bend inward.

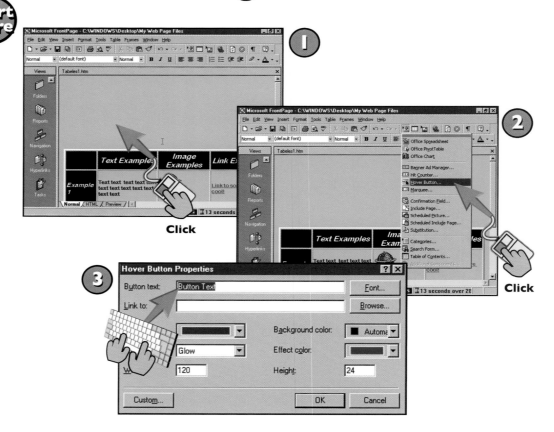

Click

Click

✓ If you want the button to lead somewhere when clicked, click the Browse button and complete the dialog box that appears just as you would complete the Create Hyperlink dialog box (see Part 5, "Making Hyperlinks") to create any other link.

✓ To see your hover buttons in action, you must save the page and then preview it in the Preview tab or in a Java-compatible browser (Internet Explorer 4 or later or Netscape Navigator 4 or later).

(1) In Page view's **Normal** tab, click where you want the button to appear.

(2) On the **Standard** toolbar, click the **Insert Component** button, and then choose **Hover Button**.

(3) Type the text you want to appear on the button.

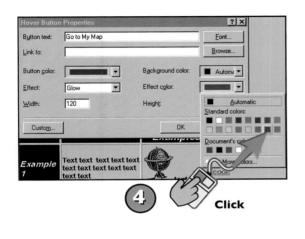

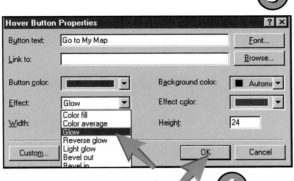

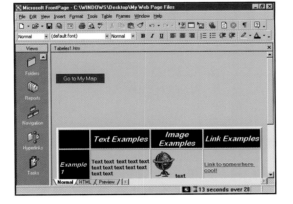

Click

Click

4 Using the lists provided, choose a **Button color** (the color of the button at rest) and an **Effect color** (the color in which the effect appears), making sure the two contrast.

5 Choose a style of **Effect** from the list.

6 Click **OK**.

✅ To change the Effect or other setting for a button, double-click it to display the Hover Button dialog box, make your changes, and click OK.

✅ Change the size, shape, or position of a hover button by performing the same steps you use to change the size, shape, or position of a picture (see Part 6) .

Task 2: Adding a Banner Ad

A *banner ad* is a spot on your page where the picture changes from one picture to another every few seconds. Banner ads are a cool and easy way to add a little *oomph* to a page, and they help hold the visitor's attention.

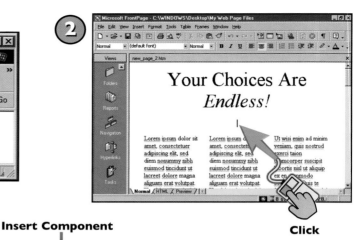

Click

Insert Component

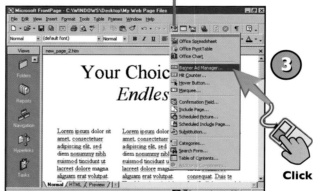

Click

✓ You must save the page to see your ad in action and then preview it in Java-compatible browser (Internet Explorer 4 or later or Netscape Navigator 4 or later). The Preview tab won't show banner ads properly.

✓ If you want the ad to lead somewhere when clicked, click the Browse button and complete the dialog box that appears.

① Plan and prepare the images you will want the banner ad to display.

② In Page view's **Normal** tab, click where you want the ad to appear.

③ On the **Standard** toolbar, click the **Insert Component** button, and then choose **Banner Ad Manager**.

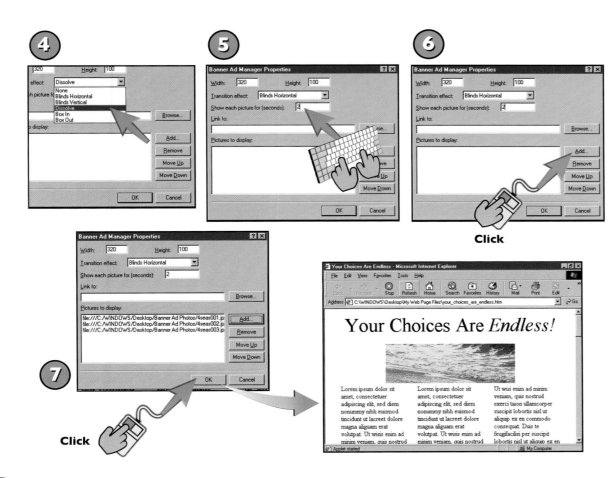

Click

Click

4 Choose a **Transition** effect to control the way one picture is changed to the next.

5 In **Show each image for (seconds)**, type the number of seconds for which each picture will show before the next.

6 Click **Add** and select the pictures to display (to change the order, select a picture in the list and click **Move Up** or **Move Down**).

7 Click **OK**.

✓ To change the Effect or other setting for an ad, double-click the ad.

✓ Change the size, shape, or position of the ad by using the same steps you use to change the size, shape, or position of a picture (see Part 6).

End Task

Task 3: Counting Visits to Your Site

On your online travels, you've no doubt seen pages that proudly report that you are the "5056th visitor" to the site, or words to that effect. That little feature is called a *hit counter*, and it does more than tell your visitors how popular you are; it helps you track your traffic.

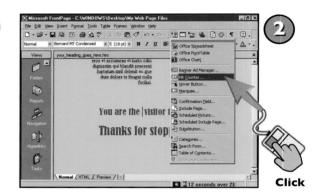

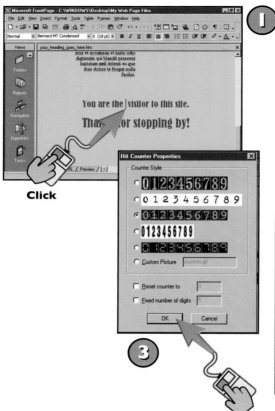

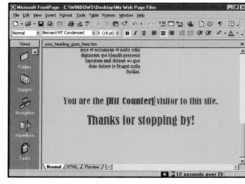

Start Here

Click

Click

Click

Click

✓ To see your counter in action, publish your page on a server that's equipped with Microsoft's FrontPage extensions. To learn whether a particular server is so equipped, talk to the system administrator.

① In Page view's **Normal** tab, click where you want the counter to appear.

② On the **Standard** toolbar, click the **Insert Component** button, and then choose **Hit Counter**.

③ Choose a **Counter Style**.

④ Click **OK**.

End Task

Task 4: Inserting a Date and Time Field

Start Here

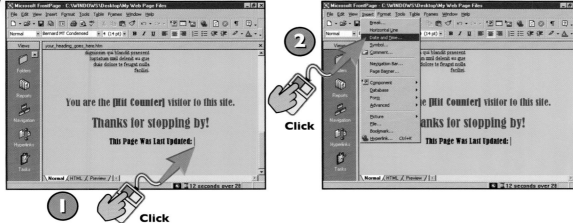

Click

Click

For some types of pages, it's helpful to visitors to report when the page or site was last updated. That way, the visitor knows whether there's anything new since his or her last visit. An automatic date and time field can help you report that information accurately.

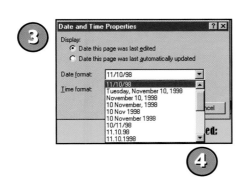

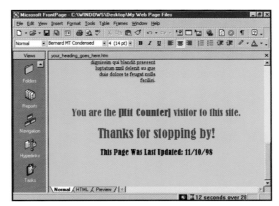

✓ In Page view, the date and time will always appear as the date and time at which you inserted the field. But online, the date and time shown will match the last time you edited the page.

1. In Page view's **Normal** tab, click where you want the date and/or time to appear.

2. Choose **Insert**, and then choose **Date and Time**.

3. Use the lists to select the **Date format** and **Time format** you want to see.

4. Click **OK**.

✓ If you have used advanced features that automatically update data in the page (not covered in this book), you can choose to show the date and/or time of the last automatic updating by choosing the Date this page was last automatically updated option.

Task 5: Making a Text Marquee Scroll Across the Page

A *marquee* is a short slice of animated text that scrolls across a Web page. The effect is like the scrolling marquee on the *New York Times* building in Manhattan, the one people in movies are always watching for bulletins during a crisis. Marquees are a fast way to add a little action to a page.

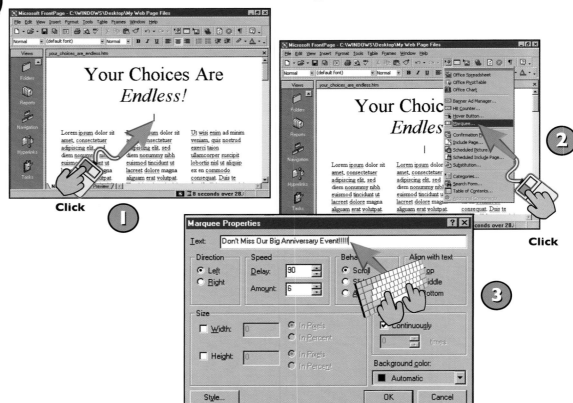

Start Here

Click

Click

At this writing, scrolling marquees are supported *only* in Internet Explorer—not in any other browser. Navigator users will see your marquee's text as regular, static text on the page. However, marquees do not require FrontPage extensions.

1 In Page view's **Normal** tab, click where you want the marquee to appear.

2 On the **Standard** toolbar, click the **Insert Component** button, and then choose **Marquee**.

3 Type the text you want to scroll across the page.

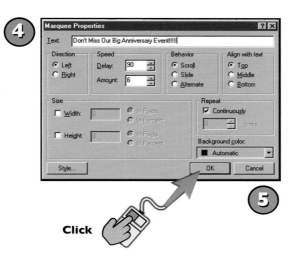

Click

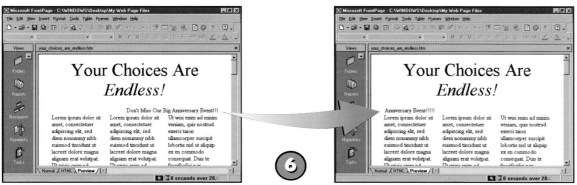

4 You can skip ahead to step 5 to use the default options for **Direction**, **Speed**, and so on, or make any changes to these settings you want.

5 Click **OK**.

6 Preview your page to see the marquee in action.

> ✓ **To change the options or text for a scrolling marquee, just double-click the marquee to open the Marquee Properties box, change whatever you like, and then click OK.**

Task 6: Adding Page Transitions

Page transitions are nifty little effects that play as a visitor arrives at a page or site, or as the visitor leaves it. Try 'em!

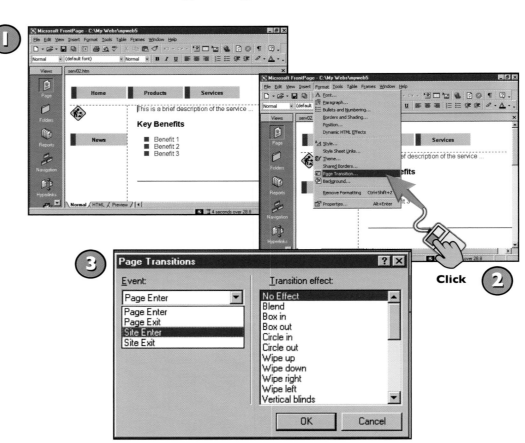

Click

If you choose Site Enter or Site Exit in step 3, the transition will show only when the visitor arrives at this page directly from another site (Site Enter) or leaves this page to go to another site (Site Exit). Going to or from another page on the same site, no transition shows.

1 In Page view's **Normal** tab, display the page to which you want to add a transition.

2 Choose **Format**, and then choose **Page Transition**.

3 From the **Event** list, choose when this transition plays: as the visitor arrives (**Page Enter**) or as he or she leaves (**Page Exit**).

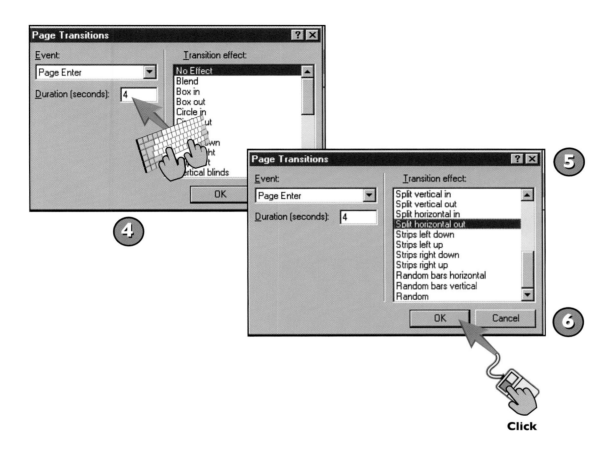

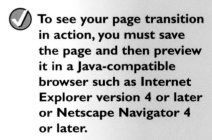

Click

In **Duration,** type the number of seconds the effect should last. (From two to five seconds is a good ballpark.)

Under **Transition Effect**, choose the effect you want.

Click **OK.**

✓ **To see your page transition in action, you must save the page and then preview it in a Java-compatible browser such as Internet Explorer version 4 or later or Netscape Navigator 4 or later.**

PART II

Adding Fill-in-the-Blanks Forms

A *form* is a part of a page that collects information from your visitors by prompting them to select options from lists, check boxes, and use other such *form fields*. When finished supplying information, the visitor clicks a Submit button to send the data to the server to be processed as you want it to be.

Creating the part of a form you **see** is easy—in fact, some of the templates include a ready-made form. But the part you see is only half of the form; the other half is the *script*, a behind-the-scenes program for collecting and processing the data that visitors enter.

How you handle the script depends on how the server where you will publish your page is equipped (see Part 12, "Publishing Your Page Online"). If the server is equipped with Microsoft software called *FrontPage extensions*, you can forget about the script and configure the form processing from within FrontPage. If not, you'll need a programmer to create a script for you.

This part shows how to add the visible parts of a form to your Web page and gets you started on dealing with the processing. But, because forms exceed the scope of an *Easy* book, I recommend that you consult closely with the administrator of the server where you will publish to set up the processing of your form.

Tasks

You can add a form to any page (as you learn to do in Task 2), or you can create a new page that already has the form in it. A great way to do that is to run FrontPage's Form Page Wizard, which custom builds a form page based on answers you give to simple questions.

Task 1: Running the Form Page Wizard

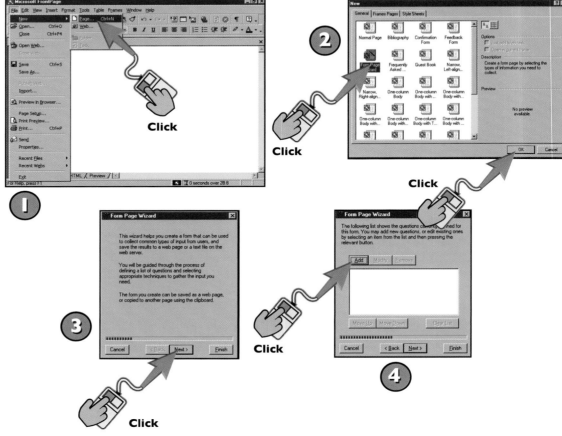

✓ Besides using the Form Page Wizard, you can start a new page or web by using a template that already has a form in it. Page templates that have their own forms include Guest Book, Feedback Form, and Confirmation form; and the Corporate Presence Wizard (see Part 9) also includes forms.

1 Start a new page by clicking **File**, **New,** and then choosing **Page**.

2 Click **Form Page Wizard**, and then click **OK**.

3 Click **Next**.

4 Click **Add**.

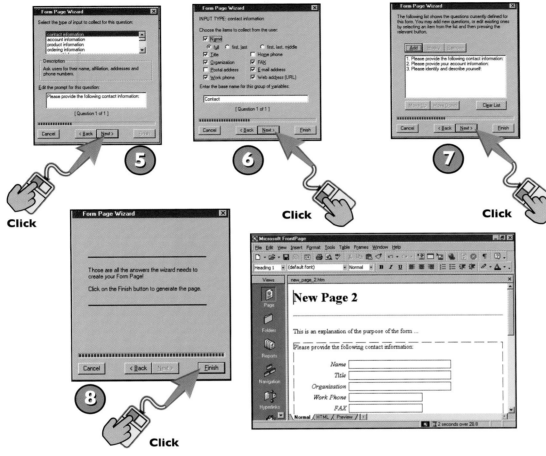

Choose one type of information to collect in the form, and then click **Next**.

Choose from any options presented, clicking **Next** after each page to advance to the next.

Repeat steps 5–7 for each type of information to collect, and then click **Next** to choose general form options.

When the wizard reports that it has no more questions, click **Finish**.

After step 7, you can change the order of the sections in the form by using the **Move Up** and **Move Down** buttons to change the order of the list.

This task demonstrates only one of the many different types of forms you can create by making different choices in the Form Page Wizard. Feel free to experiment. If you don't like the results, it's easy to start over.

The first step in building a FrontPage form from scratch is creating an invisible box in your page to hold all of the form fields. The box includes two buttons essential to any form—a Submit button that enables the visitor to submit the form data and a Reset button for clearing the form and starting over. The box also enables you to reposition the form without having to move the fields one by one.

✓ Don't worry about the size of the form box. It will expand automatically to hold whatever you put in it (performing the steps in Tasks 3–7).

Task 2: Starting a New Form from Scratch

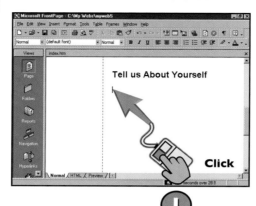

In the **Normal** tab, click in your page where you want the form to appear.

Choose **Insert**, **Form**, and then select **Form**.

Task 3: Adding the Form Fields

Start Here

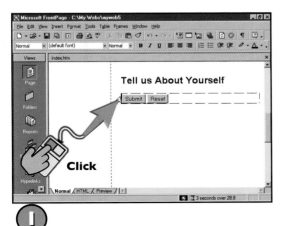

Click

Click

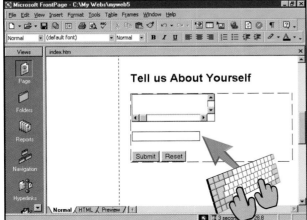

Once you've inserted the empty form with its Submit and Reset buttons, you can begin adding the form fields—the text boxes, check boxes, lists, and other doodads a visitor uses to enter information or select options. Each type of field is a little different and features different options, but inserting fields is pretty much the same.

✓ You can insert your fields above, below, or even beside the Submit and Reset buttons, but most authors leave the buttons at the very bottom of the form.

✓ Choose fields that match the input you want from the visitor. If you want a short typed response, use **One-Line Text Box**; scrolling text boxes are for longer typed responses. Radio buttons and check boxes let visitors choose one or more options shown, while a drop-down menu lets the visitor select a single item.

① Click just to the left of the Submit button to locate the edit cursor there.

② Choose **Insert**, **Form**, and then choose any of the field types shown as the top five items: from **One-Line Text Box** to **Drop-Down Menu**.

③ To insert your next field to the right of the first, repeat step 2. To insert your next field beneath the first, press **Enter** to start a new line, and then repeat step 2.

End Task

Task 4: Creating the Items on a Drop-Down Menu

To create each option a visitor can select with check boxes or radio buttons, you just add another field. But after inserting a drop-down menu, you must add to it all of the items from which the visitor can select.

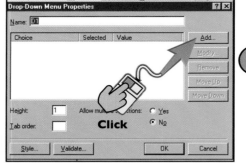

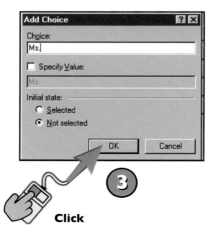

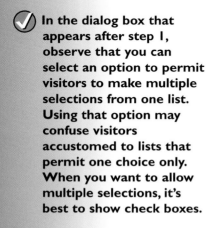

In the dialog box that appears after step 1, observe that you can select an option to permit visitors to make multiple selections from one list. Using that option may confuse visitors accustomed to lists that permit one choice only. When you want to allow multiple selections, it's best to show check boxes.

1 Double-click the drop-down menu field.

2 **Click Add**.

3 Under **Choice**, type the item text, and then click **OK**.

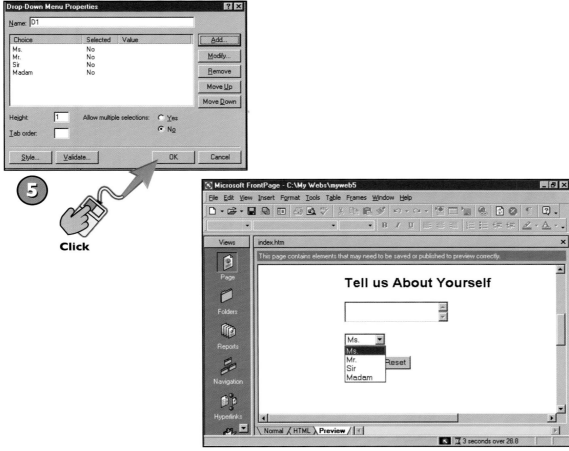

After step 5, you can rearrange the order of items in the list. In the **Drop-Down Menu Properties** dialog box, click an item whose place in the order you want to change, and then click **Move Up** or **Move Down.**

Click

④ Repeat steps 2–4 for the remaining items.

⑤ Click **OK** in the Drop-Down Menu Properties dialog box.

Task 5: Labeling the Form Fields

Of course, each form field needs an onscreen name or label so the visitor will know what to do there.

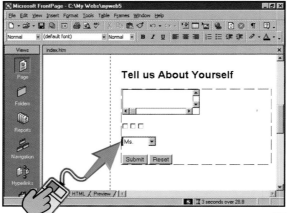

Click

✓ You can put the label anywhere you want in relation to the field (above, left, or right), as long as no other label or field comes between a label and its associated field.

① Click next to the field to locate the edit cursor there.

② Type the label text.

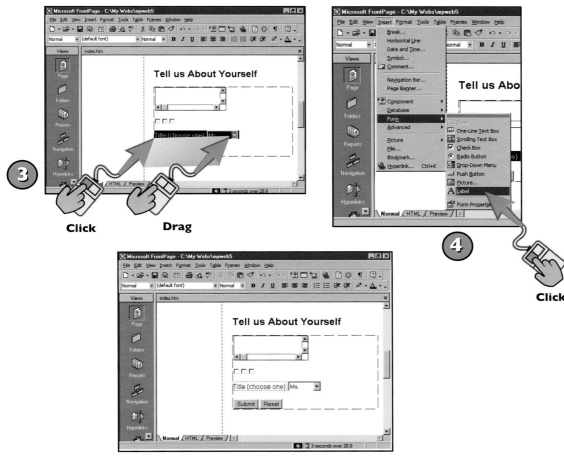

Click **Drag**

Click

3 Click and drag to select both the label and its field.

4 Choose **Insert**, **Form**, and then select **Label**.

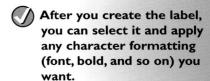
After you create the label, you can select it and apply any character formatting (font, bold, and so on) you want.

End Task

Task 6: Choosing an Initial Value for a Field

An *initial value* or *initial state* is an optional default form entry you offer your visitors to save them time. For example, if most visitors will probably choose a particular check box or menu item, you can make that option appear to be pre-selected on the form. If the visitor disagrees, he or she can change that entry. But if the initial value is what he or she would have chosen anyway, the visitor can skip that field.

✓ For a drop-down list, do step 1. In the dialog box that appears, double-click the choice you want pre-selected as the initial value, to open the **Modify Choice** dialog box. In the **Initial State** area, click the **Selected** option.

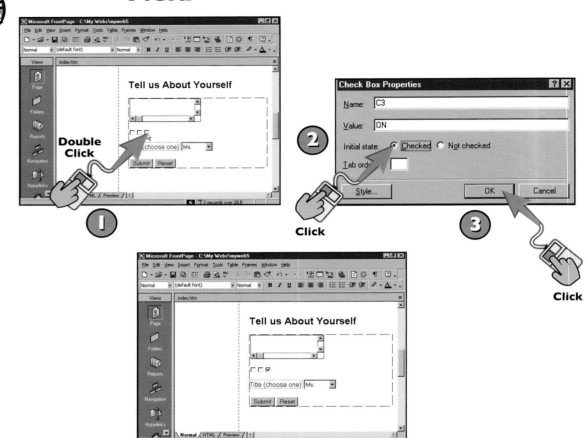

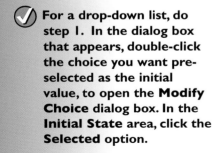

① Double-click the field for which you want to choose an initial value.

② In **Initial Value** (or **Initial State** for some field types), type or select the initial value/state.

③ Click **OK**.

Task 7: Changing Size, Shape, and Position of Fields

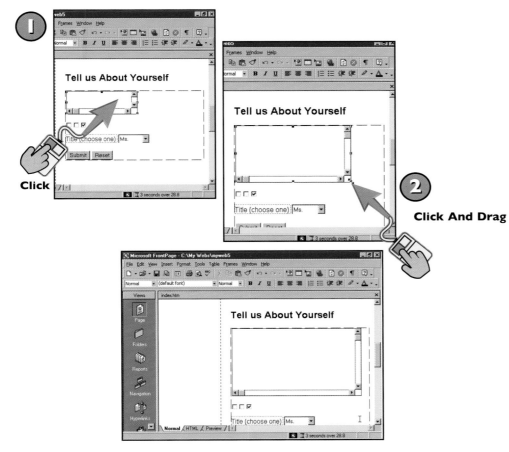

Click

Click And Drag

As a rule, treat form fields like pictures that happen to be trapped within the form box. You can drag a field or label above, below, or beside other objects, and you can use the alignment and indent buttons on the formatting toolbar to align or indent fields and labels within the form box. Beyond that, there are a few other tweaks you can use.

1. Click the field you want to modify to select it.

2. Drag the field's handles to change its size or shape, just as you would for a picture.

3. Click anywhere else to deselect the field.

✓ In a scrolling text box, you can drag top, bottom, side, or corner handles to change the size and/or shape. You can change the width of a one-line text box, but not its height; and you can change a menu's height, but not its width. Radio buttons and check boxes cannot be resized or reshaped.

Task 8: Choosing How the Form Is to Be Processed

Again, you must work closely with your Internet service provider (ISP) or the administrator of the server where you will publish your pages to set up forms processing. But the following steps can help you start that dialog.

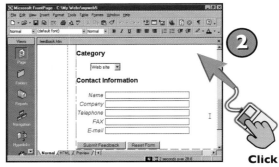

①

Contact your server administrator and ask whether the server has FrontPage extensions installed.

②

Click anywhere in the form.

③

Choose **Insert**, **Form**, and then select **Form Properties**.

✓ If the person you ask in step 1 is really the person in charge, and the answer you get is "I don't know," take that as a "No."

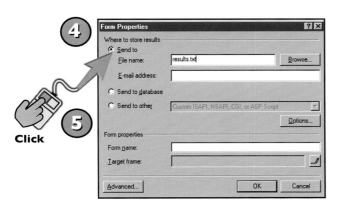

Click

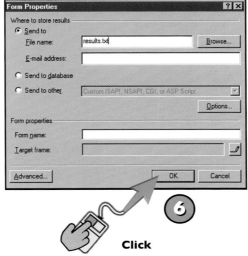

Click

4 If the server has FrontPage extensions, choose the top option, **Send to**. Enter (or Browse for) the name and location of a file in which to store form data.

5 If the server *does not* have FrontPage extensions, choose the second option, **Send to Other**, and consult with the system administrator about having a script written.

6 Click **OK**.

When the server has FrontPage extensions, you can optionally enter an email address in step 4. All form responses will be sent automatically to that address as email messages.

PART

12

Publishing Your Page Online

A play is not lines on a page. Even after it's all written and printed, it does not officially become a play until an audience sees it on stage.

Same deal with a Web page. It's not really a Web page until it gets on the Web (or at least onto your school's or company's local intranet, if that's your page's destination). In this part, you find places on the Web where you can put your pages and FrontPage webs, then how to publish them.

Tasks

Task 1: Checking Out File Sizes and Performance

FrontPage can display or print a variety of useful reports, most of which are designed to help manage large multi-author projects. But a few can help you determine the size and potential performance of your pages before publishing, so you can make adjustments if necessary. Reducing file sizes and speeding up slow pages is almost always accomplished by reducing the size and number of pictures.

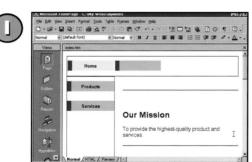

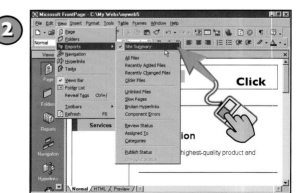

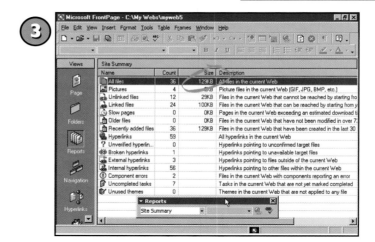

✓ If the size appears excessive, you can see the size of each file in the web by choosing **View, Reports, All Files**. Open and edit the largest files, paying particular attention to removing or reducing pictures (including picture backgrounds).

1 Open the page or web whose size and performance you want to examine.

2 Choose **View**, **Reports**, and then select **Site Summary**.

3 At the top of the **Size** column, you'll see the total number of kilobytes in the current page or web.

Next Step ▶

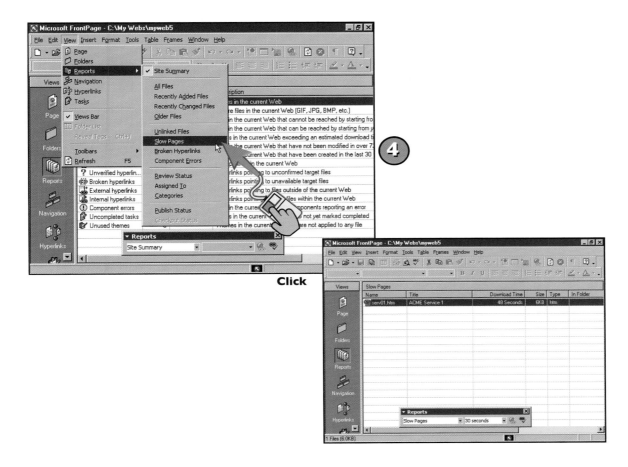

Click

You can change the criteria FrontPage uses to determine that a page is slow. Choose **Tools, Options,** and then click the Reports View tab.

While viewing any page in Page view, look in the lower-right corner of the FrontPage window to see an estimate of how long that page will take to appear at the speed of your Internet connection.

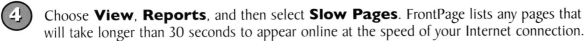

④ Choose **View**, **Reports**, and then select **Slow Pages**. FrontPage lists any pages that will take longer than 30 seconds to appear online at the speed of your Internet connection.

Task 2: Finding Space on a Web Server

To be seen by others, your pages must be stored on the hard drive of a Web server (or intranet server). Your first step is finding some server space where you will be permitted to put your pages. The following are some good ways to find that space.

Start Here

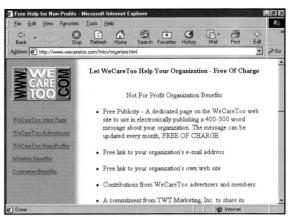

✓ If you search Yahoo! or another search tool for `free server space`, you may find companies offering free space, usually to non-profit or other worthy organizations.

✓ If your page is business- or school-related, you may find that you can publish it for free on your company's or school's Web site. Contact the administrator of that site.

(1) Check out whether you're entitled to some space on your Internet Service Provider's or online service's server.

(2) Use Yahoo! (**www.yahoo.com**) or another search tool, and use the term **web hosting** or **server space** to find companies offering space.

(3) Visit HostSearch (**www.hostsearch.com**), a Web site that helps you search for Web space providers.

Next Step

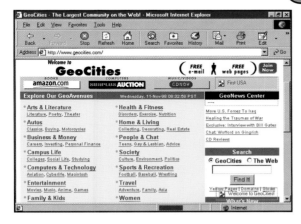

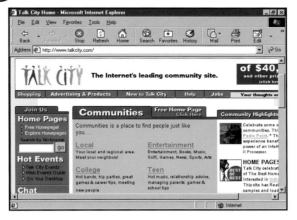

GeoCities and Talk City both require special steps for putting your page online, including the requirements that you "join" their online community first, that you include their ads on your pages, and that you follow some unusual procedures for publishing your page.

How much space? A single Web page with text and a few pictures is usually smaller than 100KB (about 1/10th of a megabyte). A web of 10 or 12 different pages may easily fit in less than a megabyte of server space. To learn the size of your page or web, see Task 1.

 Check out the "online communities" which offer free space in exchange for the right to advertise on your page:

GeoCities (**www.geocities.com**)

Talk City (**www.talkcity.com**)

Task 3: Getting Your Own *Domain*

If you simply take some space on someone else's server, your page won't have the sort of catchy Web address that gives you a Web identity, such as www.buick.com. Your page's address is expressed as a directory on the server; for example, www.serviceco.com/neddyboy/. If you want to have your own Internet name, get a domain.

☑ When typing your proposed domain name in step 3, don't precede it with the http:// or the www part. These are part of a typical Web site address, but not really part of the domain.

☑ The final part of the domain name can be .com (commercial site, the most common), .org (organization, like a foundation), .edu (educational institution), or .net (network). If you're not sure what to use, that makes you a .com.

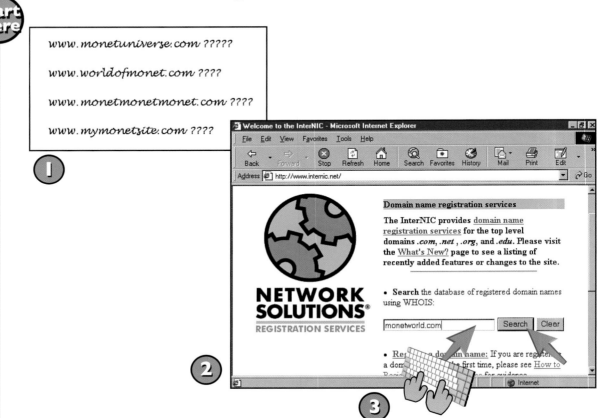

Think about what you want your Internet domain name to be; for example, www.monetmonet.com.

Visit the Web site of InterNIC, the official organization that registers Internet domains, at www.internic.net.

In the **Search** box on the InterNIC top page, type the domain name you chose in step 1, and click **Search**.

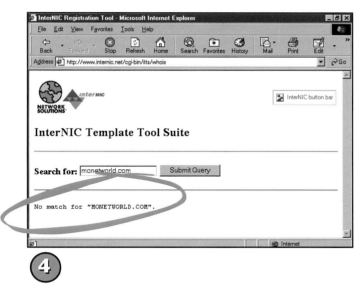

InterNIC Template Tool Suite

Search for: monetworld.com   Submit Query

No match for "MONETWORLD.COM".

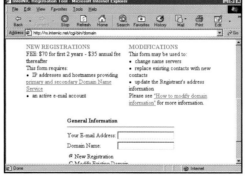

NEW REGISTRATIONS
FEE: $70 for first 2 years - $35 annual fee thereafter
This form requires:
• IP addresses and hostnames providing primary and secondary Domain Name Service
• an active e-mail account

MODIFICATIONS
This form may be used to:
• change name servers
• replace existing contacts with new contacts
• update the Registrant's address information
Please see "How to modify domain information" for more information.

General Information

Your E-mail Address:
Domain Name:
⊙ New Registration

(4) If InterNIC reports **No Match** for the domain you typed in step 3 then you can have it! Proceed to step 5. (If InterNIC displays a report all about who owns the domain, it's taken.)

(5) Contact a company that sets up domains and ask to have your chosen domain set up. You can ask your ISP to register a domain for you, or find another service by searching for **domain registration service**.

 Most ISPs will register a domain for around $50. In addition to the setup fee, the ISP will collect an additional $70 from you to pay a required registration fee to InterNIC. That pays for your domain for two years; after that, you must pay InterNIC $35 per year to keep the domain.

End Task

Task 4: Publishing from FrontPage 2000

Start
Here

Most server providers prefer that you *upload*—copy your Web files from your PC to the Web server—by using an Internet tool called *FTP*. If you're familiar with FTP, you can do it that way. But FrontPage can publish for you, so if you don't already know FTP, there's no need to learn now—at least not for publishing.

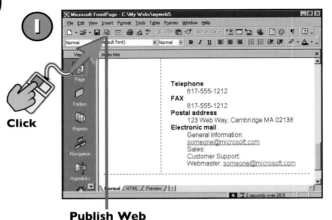

Publish Web

Click

Click

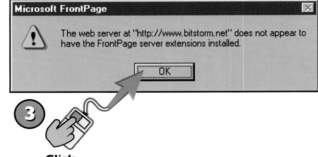

Click

✓ On some servers with the FrontPage Extensions, you may be prompted to type your username and password after step 3.

✓ If you are not connected to the Internet when you begin this task, the Wizard opens your connection dialog box when you reach a point where you need to be online.

① Open the page or web you wish to publish, and click the **Publish Web** button on the **Standard** toolbar.

② Type the address where the page will be accessed online after publishing.

③ Click **Publish**. If the server has the FrontPage extensions, you're done. If not, a message appears. Click **OK**.

Next
Step

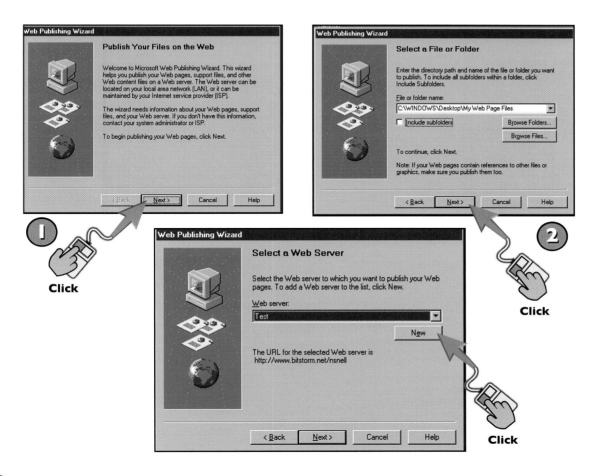

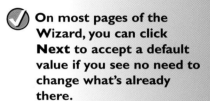

Click

Click

Click

(4) Click **Next** in the Publishing Wizard's Welcome dialog box.

(5) Click **Next**.

(6) Click **New**.

✓ **On most pages of the Wizard, you can click Next to accept a default value if you see no need to change what's already there.**

Task 4: Continued

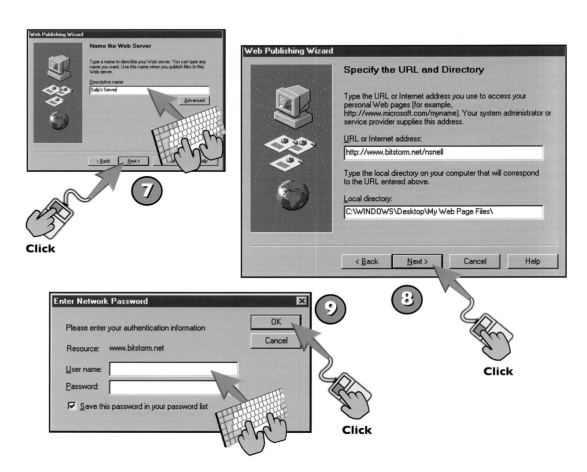

Click

Click

Click

✓ **If you get server space from your ISP, the username and password you type in step 9 will probably be the same ones you always use to connect to the Internet.**

7 Type a name (anything you want) for this server, and then click **Next**.

8 Type the URL of the server and directory where your page will be published, and then click **Next**.

9 Type the **User name** and **Password** your server supplier gave you for uploading files, and then click **OK**.

Next Step ▶

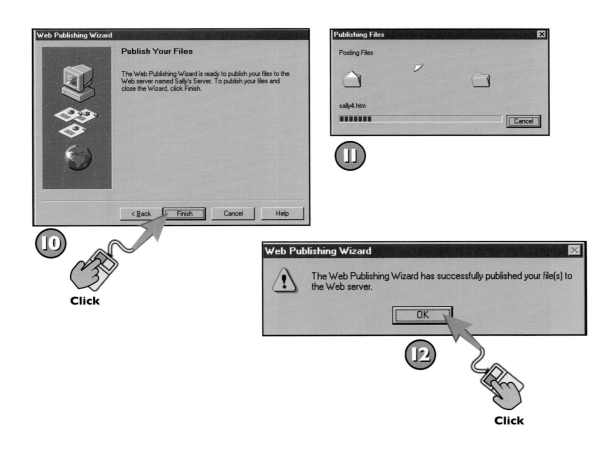

Click

Click

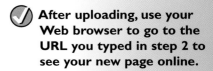

(10) Click **Finish**.

(11) Watch as the Wizard uploads your files.

(12) When the Wizard reports that it's done, click **OK**.

✅ **After uploading, use your Web browser to go to the URL you typed in step 2 to see your new page online.**

Task 5: Updating and Editing Your Page

Fixing or updating your pages after publishing them is easier than publishing them in the first place. You can't edit the copies of your pages stored on the Web server; instead, you simply make changes to the original files on your PC and publish again. The changed files automatically replace the old ones.

✓ Clicking the Publish Web button automatically reuses the settings you used before, to save time. But if you need to change those settings before publishing (to publish to a new server, for example), choose **File, Publish Web**.

✓ By default, FrontPage publishes only pages that have changed since the last time you published. If you need to republish all files, click **Options** in the Publish FrontPage dialog box, and clear the check mark next to **Published Changed Pages Only**.

Start Here

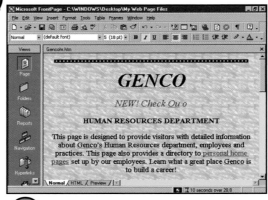

I

Publish Web

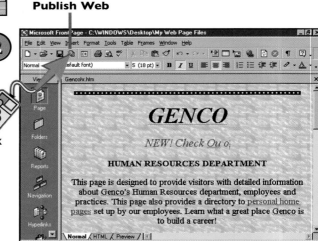

2

Click

I Edit or expand your page or web in FrontPage 2000.

2 Click the **Publish Web** button on the **Standard** toolbar. Publishing happens automatically, based on the entries you made the first time you published.

End Task

Task 6: Checking Out Site Submission Services

Start Here

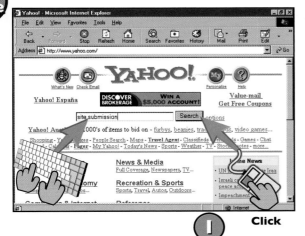

1

Click

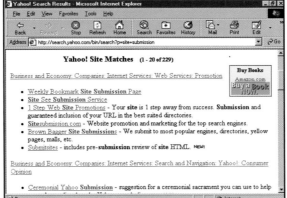

2

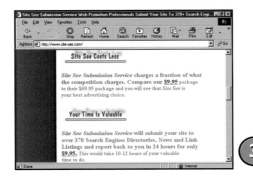

3

You can promote your site effectively by simply adding it to Yahoo! (see Task 7) and the directories on a few related pages. But for faster Web saturation, there are commercial site submission services, sometimes also known as "web promotion" firms, that will submit your site to all major search tools and other directories. The fee for the service ranges from under $10 to over $100.

✓ Browsing the Web sites of the site submission services, you can often pick up useful tips—for free—that can help you promote your site more effectively.

✓ There are also site submission packages you install on your PC. Check out a product called Submissions at www.**submissions.com**.

1. In the box at the top of the main Yahoo! page (www.yahoo.com), type **site submission** and click **Search**.

2. In the search results, read the descriptions to find sites that offer site submission.

3. Visit the sites to learn what each service offers (and what it costs).

End Task

Task 7: Listing Your Page in the Yahoo! Directory

Yahoo! is the most popular directory on the Web. It's also one that does not catalog the Web automatically—you must add your site to Yahoo! to ensure that searchers find your site when doing a Yahoo! search on a term that's related to your site's contents.

Start Here

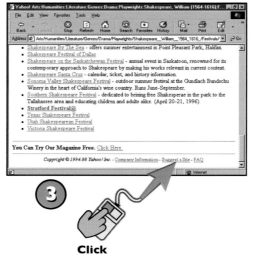

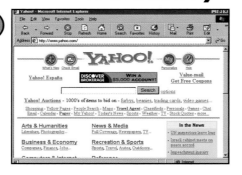

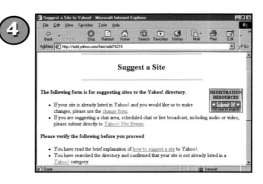

Click

✓ If the category you choose in step 2 is too broad, Yahoo! will display a message to that effect and ask you to choose another more specific category before proceeding.

① In Your Web browser, go to Yahoo at **www.yahoo.com**.

② Use Yahoo!'s search box, or browse through its category listings, to go to a category in which your site belongs.

③ Scroll to the bottom of the page on which your selected category list appears, and click **Suggest a Site**.

④ Read the Suggest a Site page for tips on properly listing your page with Yahoo!

Next Step ▶

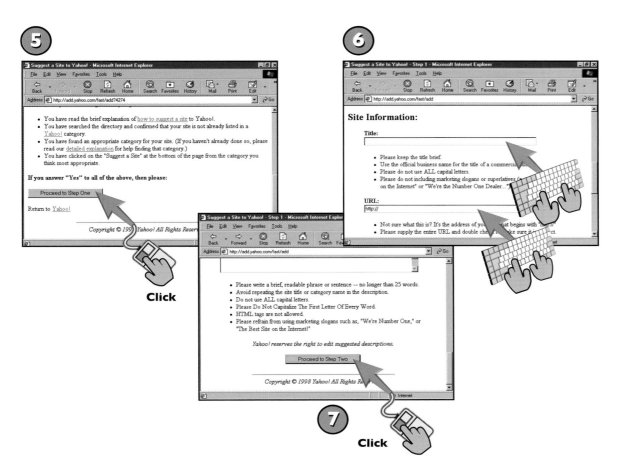

Click

Click

⑤ Scroll to the bottom of the Suggest a Site page, and click **Proceed to Step One**.

⑥ Scroll down to the **Site Information** form and type the title and URL of your page or site, plus a brief description.

⑦ At the bottom of the Suggest a Site page, click **Proceed to Step Two**. Continue through steps 2, 3 and 4, filling in all information requested and clicking the button at the bottom of the page to proceed to each new step.

✓ The description you type in step 6 will appear in the search results whenever someone's Yahoo! search finds your page. Word it carefully, to help searchers determine whether your page contains what they want. Be sure also to include in the description keywords related to the page's topic.

End Task

alignment   The way text, a picture, or a table is aligned on a page. Left-aligned objects line up to the left margin, right-aligned objects line up to the right margin, and centered objects are centered between the left and right margins.

animated GIF   A special kind of *GIF* image file that plays as a brief animated clip when viewed through a *browser*.

background   A color or image that covers the entire area behind the text and pictures of a Web page.

bookmark   An invisible marker in a Web page that provides a spot to which a link can point, so that a link can take a visitor straight to a specific spot within a page. Bookmarks are also known as targets or anchors in some Web authoring programs.

browse   To wander around the *World Wide Web* portion of the Internet, viewing files Web pages through a *browser*. Also known as surfing or cruising.

browser   A program that enables you to view Web pages, such as Microsoft Internet Explorer or Netscape Navigator.

bulleted list   A list of items in which each item is preceded by a marker, a "bullet," or some other symbol character. See also *numbered list*.

cell   The individual boxes that make up a *table*. One cell appears at each intersection of one row and one column.

CGI (Common Gateway Interface)   One method for creating scripts that make some advanced Web page features work, such as *forms*.

character formatting   Formatting that changes the style of text characters, such as applying *fonts*, bold, or italic.

check box   A small square box used to select objects in a program or a Web page *form*. Clicking an empty check box inserts a check mark there, indicating that the object or option next to the check box is selected.

clip art   Graphics, photos, and sometimes other media (such as sound and video clips) published in collections for convenient use in creating Web pages and other publications. *FrontPage 2000* includes its own library of clip art.

Clip Gallery   A program built into *FrontPage 2000* (and other *Office 2000* programs) that enables you to locate and use files stored in the *clip art* library and to add new items to that library.

collapsible list A *nested list* in which a *visitor* viewing the list through a *browser* can choose to display or hide ("collapse") nested list items by clicking the major list items.

component An object in a Web page that carries out a programmed action; components include hit counters, *marquees*, and *form* fields.

Dynamic HTML (DHTML) A set of technologies, including style sheets and scripting languages like JavaScript, that enables a Web page to include a variety of advanced interactive features and design. (DHTML features function only when the page is viewed through a DHTML-compatible browser.)

dialog box A box that pops up in Windows programs to provide the options necessary for completing a particular task. Different tasks display different dialog boxes.

download The act of copying information from a server computer to your computer. See also *upload*.

domain The address of a computer on the Internet. A user's Internet address is made up of a username and a domain name. Every Web server has its own unique domain and can play host to other domains as well.

email address The Internet address used in an email program to send email to a particular Internet user. The address is typically made up of a username, an @ sign, and a domain name (user@domain).

FAQ file Short for *Frequently Asked Questions file*. A computer file, often made available on the Internet, containing the answers to frequently asked questions about a particular topic or Web site.

folder list A tree of folders and files displayed in *Navigation view* to help you see and work with the organization of a *FrontPage Web*.

font A particular style of text.

font size The relative size in which text appears onscreen.

form A part of a Web page in which users can type entries or make selections that are then collected and processed. Forms require either the *FrontPage extensions* or a *script* on the server.

frames Multiple panes in a browser window, each of which displays a different Web page file. Web authors design frames pages to enable visitors to use the frames together as a single, multidimensional Web page.

FrontPage 2000 A Web-page authoring and publishing program for Windows (95/98/NT) from Microsoft, sold by itself and also included in the Premium edition of the *Office 2000* suite.

FrontPage extensions   A set of programs that, when installed on a Web *server*, enable *forms* and some *components* in Web pages created in *FrontPage 2000* to perform their tasks without the aid of a *script*.

FrontPage Web   A group of Web page files designed, edited, and managed in FrontPage to work together as a *Web site*.

FTP   Short for *File Transfer Protocol*. The basic method for copying a file from one computer to another through the Internet. Often used for publishing Web page files by *uploading* them to a server.

GIF   Short for *Graphics Interchange Format*. A form of computer image file using the file extension .GIF, commonly used for *inline images* in Web pages.

heading   A short line of text, often set large and bold, that marks the start of a particular section of a document, such as a Web page.

highlight color   A transparent band of color laid over selected text in a Web page to call attention to the text.

horizontal line   In a Web page, a straight line that divides sections of the page horizontally. Sometimes also known as a horizontal rule.

hotspot   In *FrontPage 2000*, a region within the area of a picture in a Web page. Web authors may define multiple hotspots within a single picture, so that clicking different parts of the picture activates different links.

HTML (Hypertext Markup Language)   The document formatting language used to create Web pages. The files produced by Web authoring programs like *FrontPage 2000* are HTML files.

hyperlink   See *link*.

inline image   An picture that appears within the layout of a Web page.

Internet   A large, loosely organized internetwork connecting universities, research institutions, governments, businesses, and other organizations so that they can exchange messages and share information.

Internet Explorer   A *browser* for the World Wide Web, created by Microsoft. Internet Explorer version 4 is built into Windows 98 and available free for other systems.

intranet   An internal network in a company, school, or other organization that is based on Internet technologies so that using it is just like using a *browser* on the *World Wide Web*.

Java   A programming language that can be used to create applets—programs that run inside a Web *browser*.

JavaScript   A method for creating *scripts* that make some advanced Web page features work, such as *forms*.

JPEG   A form of image file, using the file extension .JPG (or .jpeg), commonly used for *inline images* in Web pages.

link   Short for *hyperlink*, an object in a Web page that takes the visitor to another page, downloads a file, or starts some other action.

link source   The part of a link that a visitor actually sees in a Web page and clicks to activate the link. (The other part of a link is the *URL*.) A link source can be some text, an *inline image*, or a *hotspot*.

list box   In a *dialog box* or Web page form, a small box with a downward-pointing arrow at its right end. Clicking the arrow opens a list of options the user can click to select one to appear in the box.

mailto link   A link in a Web page that, when clicked by a visitor, opens the visitor's email program and creates a new message pre-addressed to a particular person.

marquee   A line of text that repeatedly scrolls across part of a Web page, used as an attention-getting device.

menu   A list of choices on a computer screen. A user selects one choice to perform an action with a software program.

Navigation view   A version of the *FrontPage 2000* window displayed when the user clicks the Navigation button in the *Views bar*. Used for managing a *FrontPage Web*.

Navigator   Sometimes called *Netscape*, a popular *browser* from Netscape Communications. Navigator is available in a suite called Netscape Communicator that also includes programs for Web authoring, email, and other activities.

nested list   A multilevel *bulleted list* or *numbered list* in which some list items are indented to form sub-lists under the item above them, as in an outline.

Netscape   Short for Netscape Communications Corporation, a software company that developed and markets the Netscape *Navigator Web browser*. Some people casually refer to Navigator as "Netscape."

network   A set of computers interconnected so that they can communicate and share information. Connected networks together form an internetwork.

numbered list   A list of items in which each item is preceded by a number, and the numbers go up as the list goes down. See also *bulleted list*.

Office 2000   A suite of application programs from Microsoft, available in several versions. The Premium version for Windows 95/98/NT includes *FrontPage 2000*, Word, Excel, and other popular programs.

page transition   An animated effect that plays when a visitor moves between two pages in a *FrontPage Web*.

paragraph   Any block of text uninterrupted by a paragraph mark (¶).

paragraph break   The space between two paragraphs in which a hidden paragraph mark appears.

paragraph formatting   Text formatting, such as *paragraph styles* or *alignment*, that can be applied only to a whole paragraph or paragraphs, never to only selected characters within a paragraph, like *character formatting*.

paragraph style   The principal form of text formatting on a Web page. Paragraph styles include six levels of *headings*, a style for normal text, and several different styles for creating lists.

position box   A feature of *Dynamic HTML* that enables a Web author to precisely position a picture or other object within the area of a Web page.

script   A program, written in *JavaScript*, VB Script, Perl, or another such language, that can be invoked from a Web page to perform a particular task, such as processing a *form*.

search engine   A program, often accessed through a Web page, that provides a way to search for specific information, such as *Yahoo!*.

selection   Text or a picture that the author has highlighted so that the next action the author performs affects only the highlighted text or picture.

server   A computer on a network, used to store information and "serve" it to other computers that contact it through the network. A Web server stores Web pages that it serves to the browsers that contact it through the Internet.

shareware   Software programs that users are permitted to acquire and evaluate for free. Shareware is different from freeware in that, if a person likes the shareware program and plans to use it on a regular basis, he or she is expected to send a fee to the programmer.

signature   A block of text on a Web page, usually near the bottom, that identifies the page's author or the *Webmaster*. Signatures often include a *mailto link* to the author's *email address*.

style   See *paragraph style*.

style sheet   A technology that enables a Web author to more precisely control the appearance of a Web page and to easily apply and modify that design in multiple pages.

symbol   A character that's not on the keyboard, such as a copyright symbol. In *FrontPage 2000*, you add symbols to your pages from a special *dialog box*.

table   A box or grid used to arrange text or pictures in neat rows and columns; often used in *FrontPage 2000* to organize the entire layout of the page.

tag   A code in the *HTML* language.

task   In *FrontPage 2000*, an activity assigned to an individual as part of coordinating a multi-author Web authoring project, usually over a *network* on which *FrontPage 2000* is installed.

template A preformatted Web page (containing sample text and pictures) that a Web author copies and edits to conveniently create a new page.

theme In *FrontPage 2000,* a set of formatting instructions governing the *background, fonts,* colors, and button styles in a page. Themes provide a fast way to design a page or change a design and to apply a matching design to multiple pages in a *FrontPage Web.*

title The name that identifies a particular Web page. A Web page's title appears in the title bar at the very top of the *browser* window.

toolbar In a program, a row of icons or buttons, usually near the top of the program's window, that you can click to perform common tasks.

Undo A feature of *FrontPage* and some other programs that enables you to reverse an action you performed if you change your mind.

upload The act of copying information to a server computer from your computer. See also *download.*

URL Short for *uniform* (or *universal*) *resource locator.* A method of standardizing the addresses of different types of Internet resources so that they can all be accessed easily from within a Web browser.

Views bar In *FrontPage 2000,* a vertical bar along the left side of the window, used to switch between different versions of the window, each designed for a different activity.

visitor A casual way a Web author may refer to the people who will access his or her creations through the *Internet* or an *intranet.*

Visual Basic A multipurpose programming language from Microsoft, often used for Web page *scripts* and for automating tasks in *Office 2000* programs.

Web See *FrontPage Web* or *World Wide Web.*

Webmaster The person responsible for the management and maintenance of a particular Web page or Web site. Sometimes (but not always) also the Web page's author.

Web site A group of individual Web pages linked together into a single, multipage document. The term Web site also is sometimes used to describe a whole Web *server* or all pages on a particular *domain.*

wizard Automated routines, used throughout Windows, for conveniently performing a step-by-step procedure, such as installing *FrontPage 2000.*

World Wide Web (WWW or Web) A set of Internet computers and services that provides an easy-to-use system for finding information and moving among resources. Do not confuse with *FrontPage Web.*

Yahoo! A popular search engine.

Symbols

CD icon

forms

G - H

I

links

M

N - O

P

Web pages

Notes